ESTATE PUBLICATIONS

STEVENAGE · LETCHWORTH

BALDOCK · HITCHIN

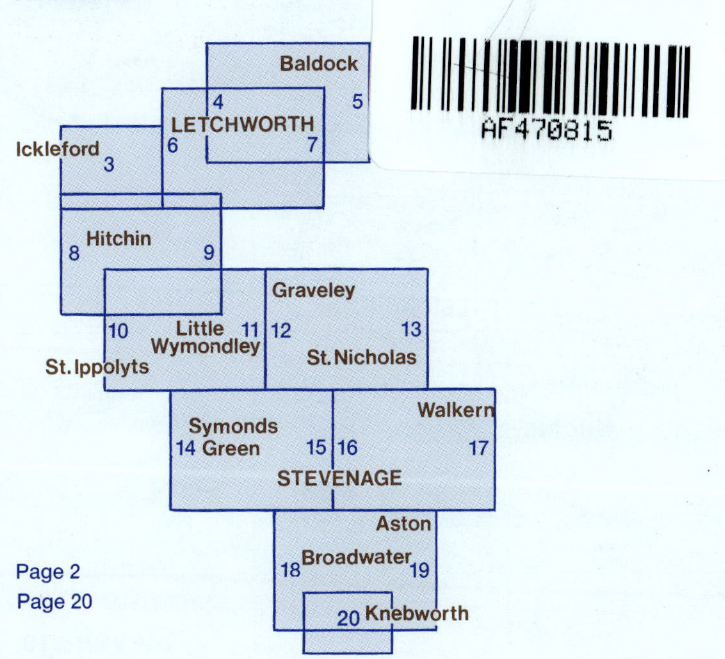

ROAD MAP   Page 2
STREET INDEX Page 20

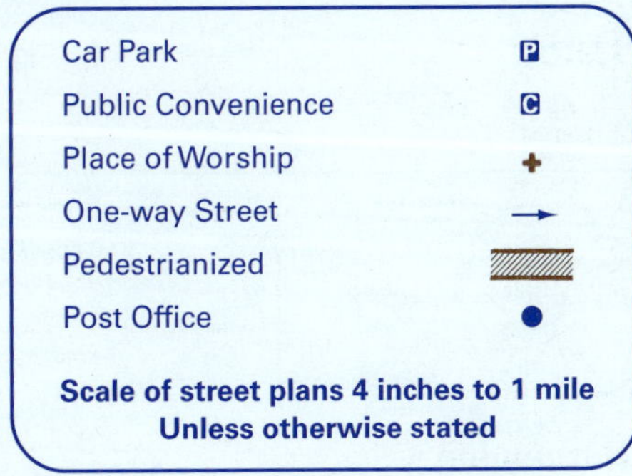

Every effort has been made to verify
the accuracy of information in this
book but the publishers cannot accept
responsibility for expense or loss
caused by an error or omission.
Information that will be of assistance
to the user of the maps will be welcomed.

The representation on these maps of a
road, track or path is no evidence of the
existence of a right of way.

Car Park	P
Public Convenience	C
Place of Worship	+
One-way Street	→
Pedestrianized	
Post Office	●

Scale of street plans 4 inches to 1 mile
Unless otherwise stated

Street plans prepared and published by ESTATE PUBLICATIONS, Bridewell House, TENTERDEN, KENT.
The Publishers acknowledge the co-operation of the local authorities
of towns represented in this atlas.

Ordnance Survey® This product includes mapping data licensed from Ordnance Survey®
with the permission of the Controller of Her Majesty's Stationery Office.

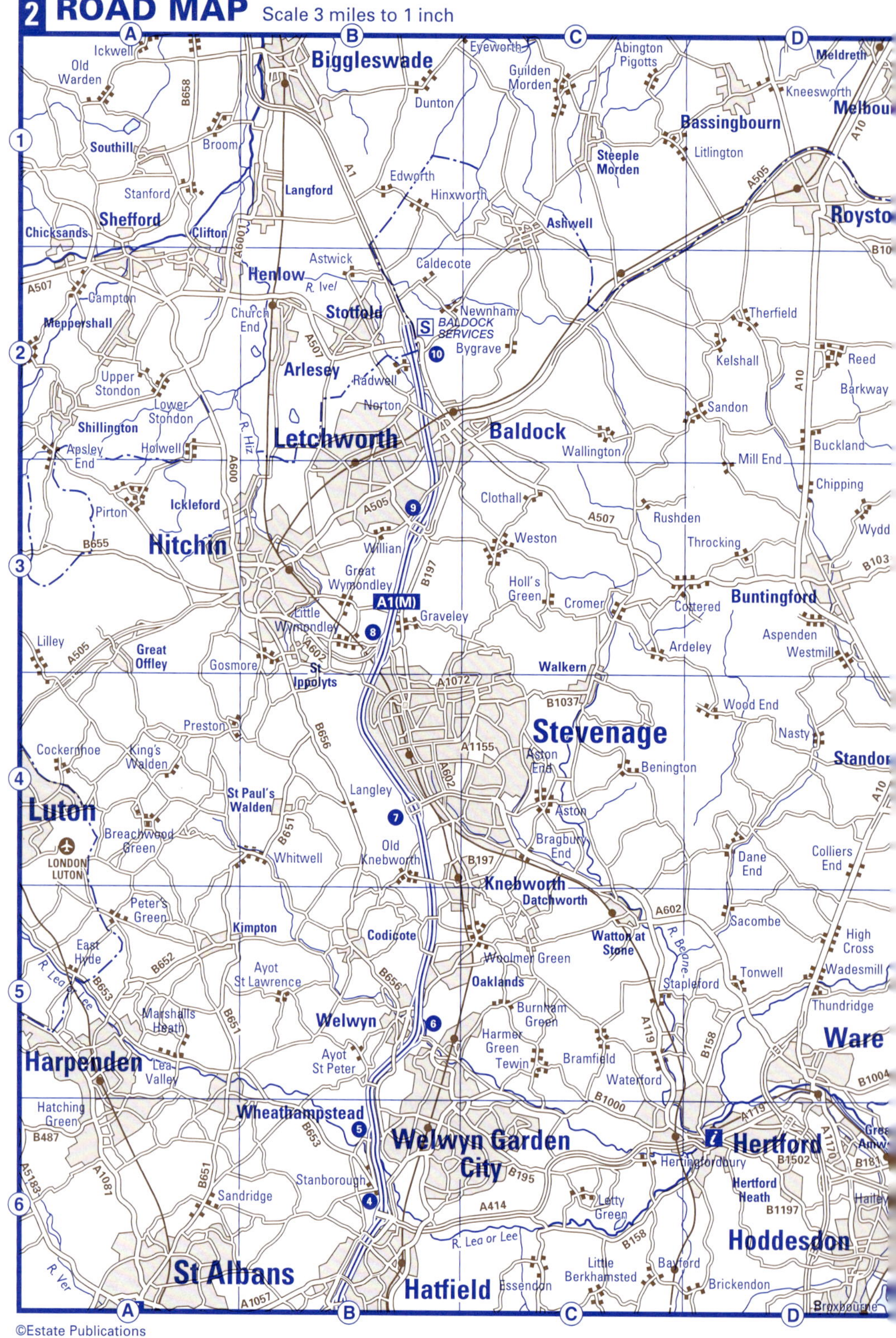

2 ROAD MAP   Scale 3 miles to 1 inch
A B C D
1
Ickwell
Old Warden
Southill
Broom
Stanford
Shefford
Chicksands
Clifton
A6001
B658
A507
A507
Campton
Meppershall
Upper Stondon
Lower Stondon
Shillington
Apsley End
Holwell
Pirton
Ickleford
Hitchin
B655
A600
A505
R. Hiz
Henlow
Astwick
R. Ivel
Stotfold
Arlesey
Radwell
Norton
Letchworth
Langford
Biggleswade
Eyeworth
Dunton
Edworth
Hinxworth
Ashwell
Caldecote
Newnham
Bygrave
BALDOCK SERVICES
S
10
Baldock
Wallington
Clothall
Weston
Holl's Green
Cromer
A505
A507
Willian
Great Wymondley
Little Wymondley
Graveley
A1(M)
B197
9
8
Guilden Morden
Abington Pigotts
Steeple Morden
Litlington
A505
Bassingbourn
Therfield
Kelshall
Reed
Barkway
Sandon
Buckland
Mill End
Chipping
Wydd
Rushden
Throcking
Cottered
Buntingford
Aspenden
Westmill
Ardeley
Meldreth
Kneesworth
Melbou
Roysto
A10
A505
B103
B103
Lilley
Great Offley
Gosmore
St Ippolyts
A505
A602
B656
Preston
Cockernhoe
King's Walden
Luton
St Paul's Walden
Langley
Old Knebworth
Stevenage
A1072
A1155
B1037
Aston End
Benington
Wood End
Nasty
Standor
Walkern
7
A602
Breachwood Green
LONDON LUTON
Peter's Green
Whitwell
Kimpton
Codicote
Woolmer Green
Knebworth
Datchworth
Aston
Bragbury End
Watton at Stone
A602
Dane End
Colliers End
Sacombe
A10
East Hyde
R. Lea & Lee
B652
B653
Ayot St Lawrence
B651
Marshalls Heath
Welwyn
Ayot St Peter
Oaklands
Burnham Green
Harmer Green
Tewin
Bramfield
High Cross
Wadesmill
Stapleford
Tonwell
Thundridge
A119
B158
Ware
B1004
6
Harpenden
Lea Valley
Hatching Green
B487
A5183
A1081
Sandridge
Wheathampstead
5
Welwyn Garden City
Stanborough
4
A414
B653
B651
B656
B195
Waterford
B1000
Letty Green
A119
Hertford
Hertingfordbury
B1502
B181
Hertford Heath
B158
Hoddesdon
St Albans
A1057
Hatfield
Essendon
Little Berkhamsted
Bayford
Brickendon
B1197
A1170
Gres Amw
Hailey
Broxbourne
R. Ver
A1072
1
2
3
4
5
6

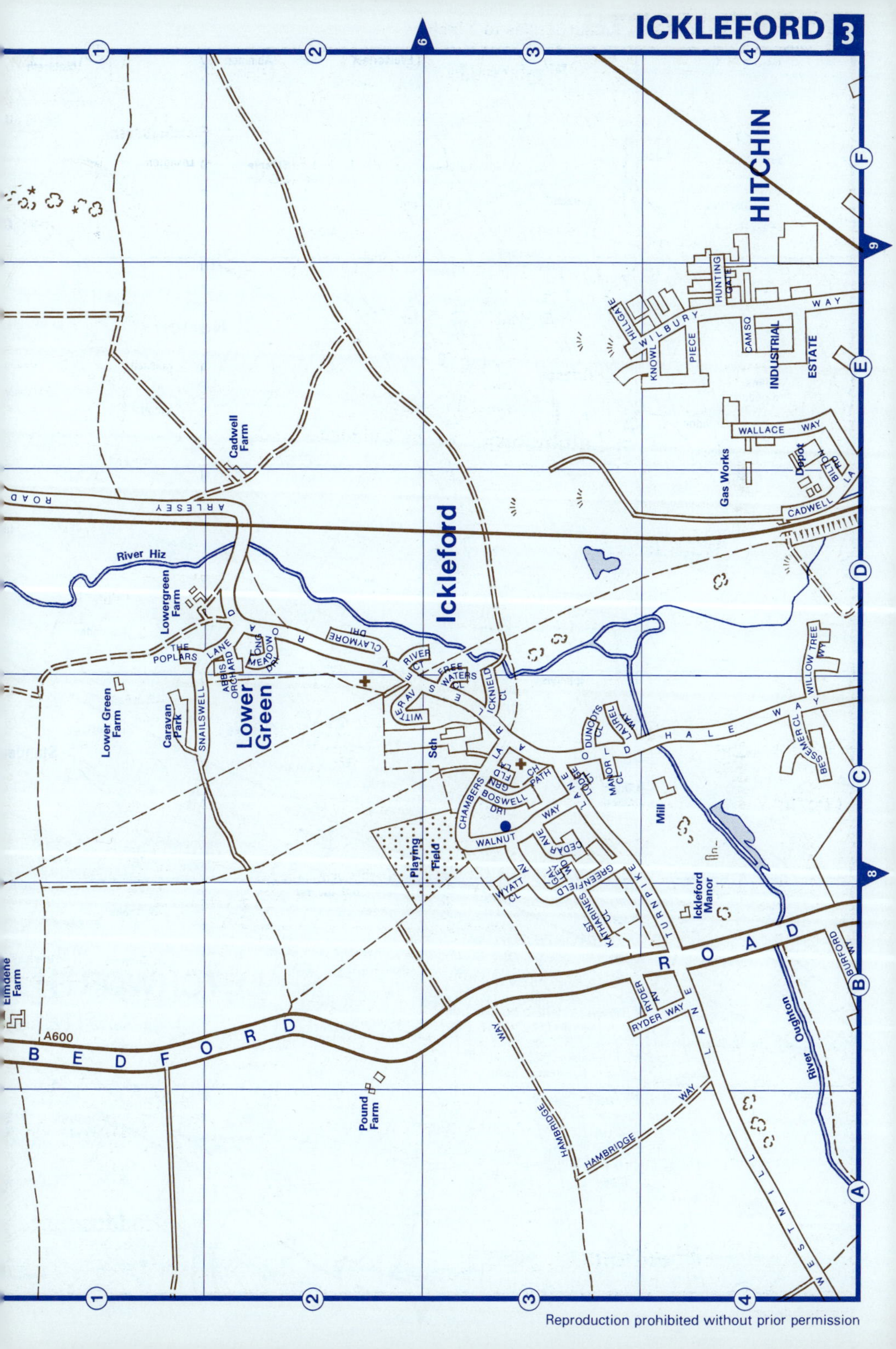

ICKLEFORD
3
HITCHIN
1
2
6
3
4
5
9
F
E
D
C
B
A
8
HILLGATE
KNOWL PIECE
WILBURY
HUNTING GATE
CAM SQ
INDUSTRIAL
ESTATE
WAY
WALLACE WAY
Gas Works
Depot
BILTON RD
CADWELL LA
Cadwell Farm
ARLESEY
ROAD
River Hiz
Lowergreen Farm
THE POPLARS
Lower Green Farm
Caravan Park
SNAILSWELL LANE
ABBIS ORCHARD
MEADOW DRI
CLAYMORE DRI
Ickleford
Lower Green
Sch
WITHERAV
RIVER
CT
FREE
WATERS CL
ICKNIELD
CL
WILLOW TREE WY
BEMER CL
BESSEMER CL
HALE WAY
LAUREL
WAY
MANOR CL
DUNCOTS
CL
LODGE
LANE
BARL AV
GDN FLD
CH
PATH
CHAMBERS
BOSWELL DRI
WALNUT
Playing Field
WYATT CL
ST KATHARINES CL
CEDAR WY
GAL LANE
GREENFIELD
TURNPIKE LANE
Mill
Ickleford Manor
RYDER AV
RYDER WAY
ROAD
BURFORD WY
River Oughton
WESTMILL
HAMBRIDGE WAY
HAMBRIDGE LANE
Pound Farm
BEDFORD
ROAD
A600
Elmdene Farm
Reproduction prohibited without prior permission

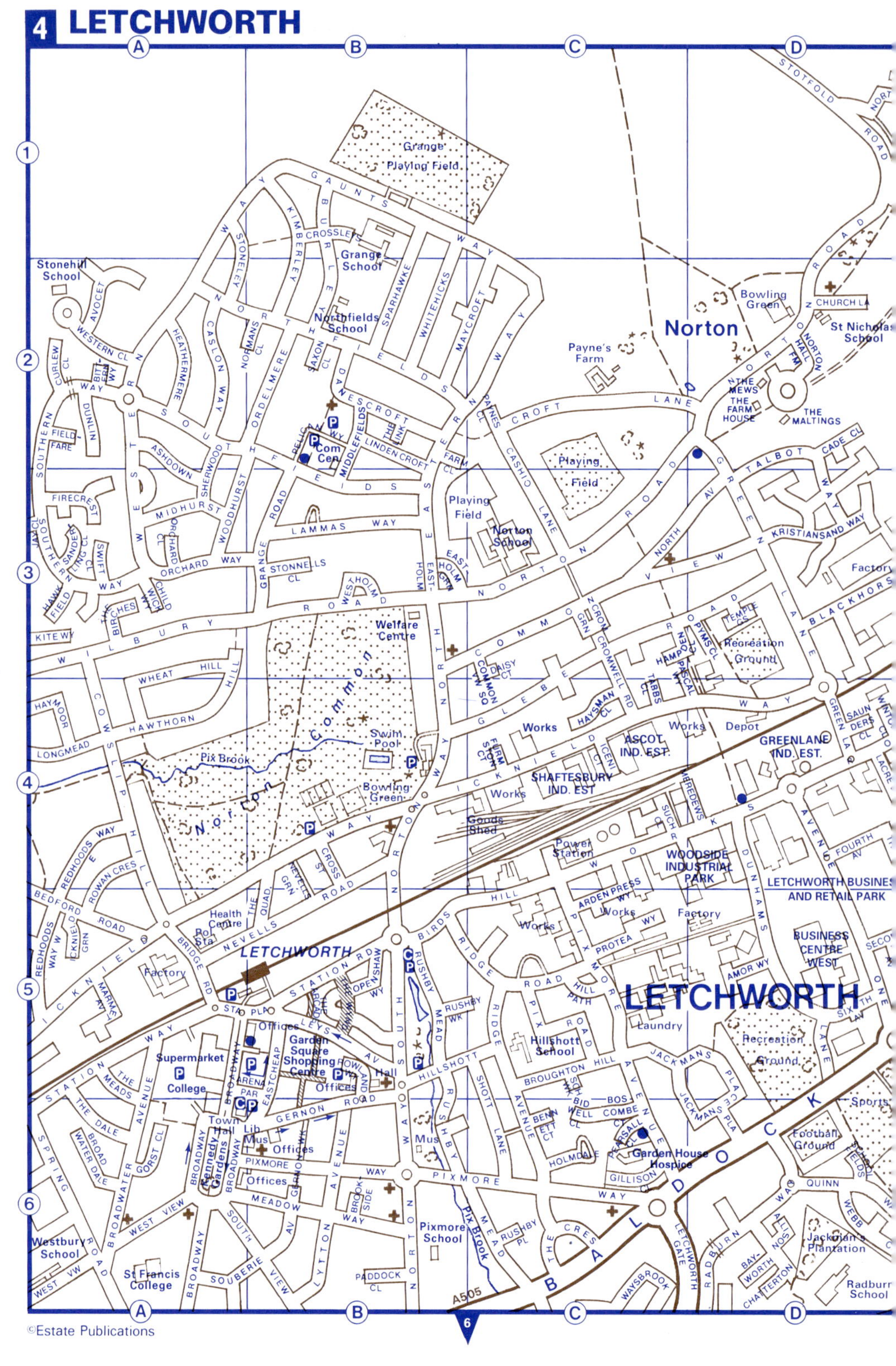
LETCHWORTH
Norton
Stotfold Road
Grange Playing Field
Stonehill School
Grange School
Northfields School
St Nicholas School
Bowling Green
Church La
Payne's Farm
The Mews
The Farm House
The Maltings
Com Cen
Playing Field
Norton School
Playing Field
Welfare Centre
Recreation Ground
Factory
Ascot Ind. Est.
Shaftesbury Ind. Est.
Works
Works
Depot
Greenlane Ind. Est.
Swim. Pool
Pix Brook
Bowling Green
Goods Shed
Power Station
Woodside Industrial Park
Letchworth Business and Retail Park
Business Centre West
Health Centre
Letchworth
Hillshott School
Laundry
Recreation Ground
Supermarket
College
Garden Square Shopping Centre
Offices
Town Hall
Mus
Offices
Kennedy Gardens
Garden House Hospice
Football Ground
Jackson's Plantation
Westbury School
St Francis College
Pixmore School
Radburn School
Estate Publications

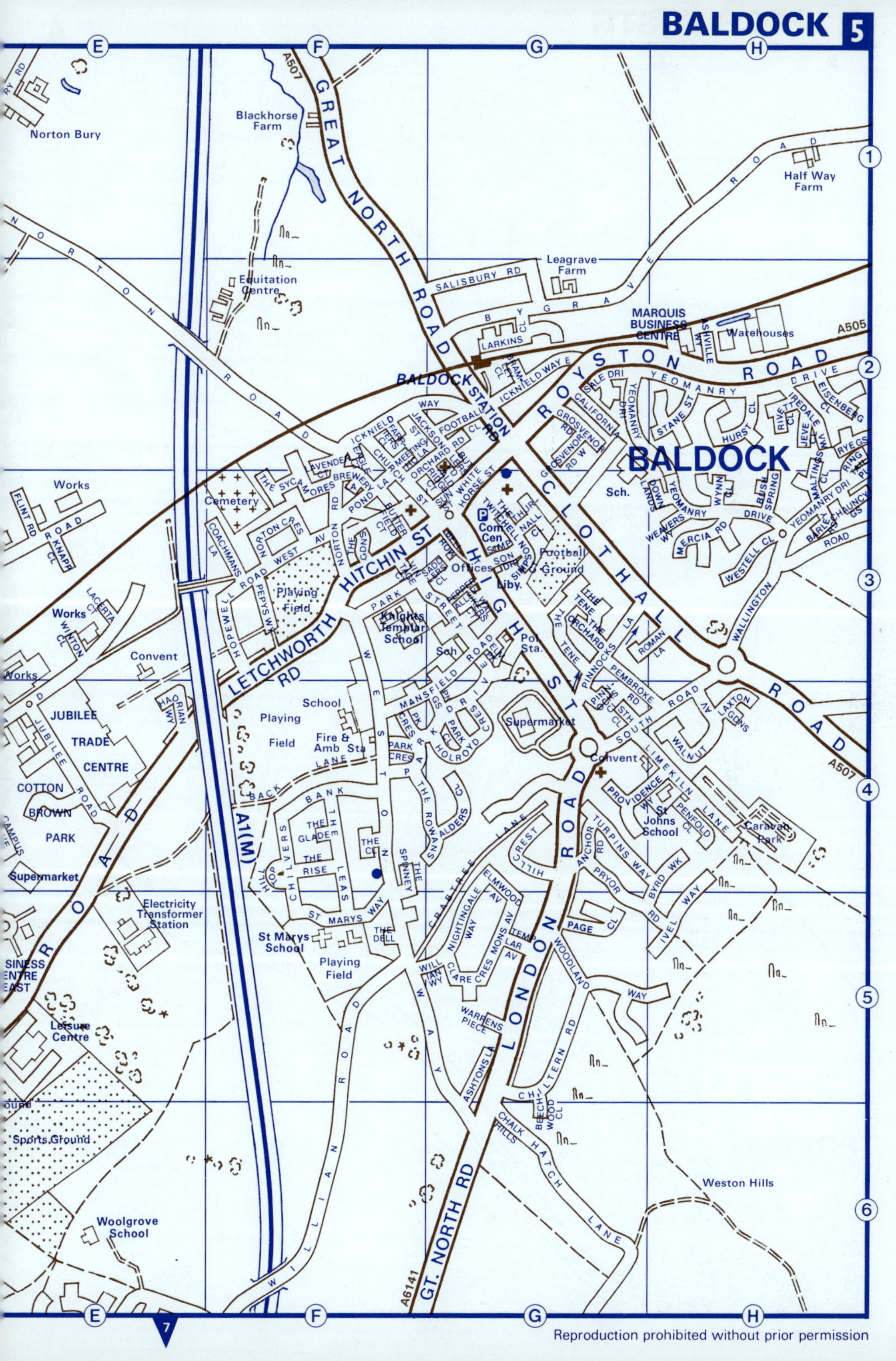

BALDOCK 5
Norton Bury
Blackhorse Farm
Half Way Farm
GREAT NORTH ROAD
A507
Equitation Centre
Leagrave Farm
SALISBURY RD
MARQUIS BUSINESS CENTRE
Warehouses
A505
BALDOCK STATION
ROYSTON ROAD
Larkins
ICKNIELD WAY
BALDOCK
Sch.
Works
FLINT RD
KNAPP CL
ROAD
Cemetery
THE SYCAMORES
BREWERY LA
NORTON RD
Playing Field
LETCHWORTH RD
HITCHIN ST
HIGH ST
CLOTHALL ROAD
WALLINGTON
Works
WINTON CL
LACERTA CT
Convent
Knights Templar School
Sch
Football Ground
Offices
Liby.
Pol. Sta.
ROMAN LA
Works
JUBILEE TRADE CENTRE
COTTON
BROWN PARK
Supermarket
HADRIAN WY
A1(M)
School
Playing Field
Fire & Amb Sta
Mansfield Road
Supermarket
Convent
St Johns School
Caravan Park
PROVIDENCE WY
LIMEKILN LANE
WALNUT
Electricity Transformer Station
THE GLADE
THE RISE
CHILVERS
THE SPINNEY
ST MARYS WAY
St Marys School
THE DELL
Playing Field
LONDON ROAD
WARRENS PIECE
ASHTONS LA
Leisure Centre
Sports Ground
Woolgrove School
GT. NORTH RD
A6141
Weston Hills
CHALK HATCH HILLS
Reproduction prohibited without prior permission

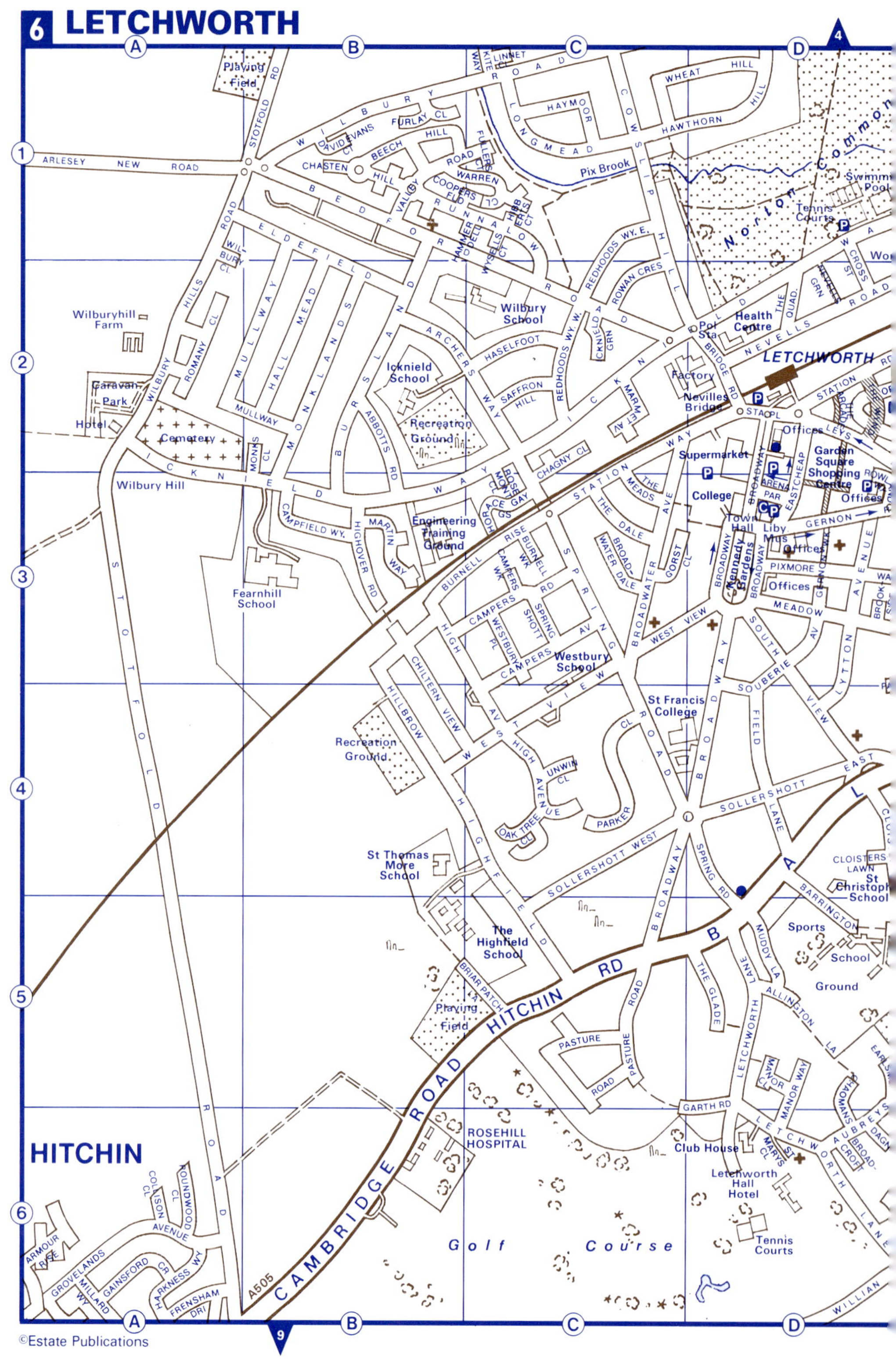

6 LETCHWORTH
HITCHIN
Playing Field
ARLESEY NEW ROAD
STOTFOLD RD
WILLBURY ROAD
DAVID EVANS CT
CHASTEN HILL
FURLAY CL
BEECH HILL
VALLEY
COOPERS FLD
WARREN
WILBURY HILLS
ELDEFIELD
ROMANY CL
MULLWAY
HALL MEAD
MONKLANDS
BEDFOR
ICKNIELD
MONKS CL
CAMPFIELD WY.
HIGHOVER RD
MARTIN WAY
ABBOTTS RD
BURY WAY
ARCHERS WAY
HASELFOOT
SAFFRON HILL
MART
WYSELLS CT
HIBBERTS CTLS
HAMMER DELL
BUNGALOW
DELL
FULLERS ROAD
KITE WAY
LINNET CL
LONGMEAD
HAYMOOR
COWSLIP
HILL
REDHOODS WY. W.
ROWAN CRES
REDHOODS WY. E.
ICKNIELD GRN
MARMET
KING
WHEAT HILL
HAWTHORN
HILL
Pix Brook
Norton Common
Swimming Pool
Tennis Courts
THE QUAD
NEVELLS
CROSS ST
Wilbury School
Pol Sta
Health Centre
LETCHWORTH
BRIDGE RD
Factory
Nevilles Bridge
STA PL
STATION
ARCHERS
Offices
LEYS
Supermarket
Garden Square Shopping Centre
Offices
College
BROADWAY
EASTCHEAP PAR
ARENA
CP
GERNON
Town Hall
Liby
Mus
Offices
Kennedy Gardens
BROADWAY
PIXMORE
Offices
AVENUE
MEADOW
Wilburyhill Farm
Caravan Park
Hotel
Cemetery
Wilbury Hill
STOTFOLD ROAD
Icknield School
Recreation Ground
Engineering Training Ground
ROSE GAY
HORACE
BURNELL RISE
CAMPERS WK
BURNELL WK
SHOTT
SPRING RD
CHAGNY CL
STATION
THE MEADS
THE DALE
WATER DALE
BROADWATER
GORST CL
WEST VIEW
SOUTH AVE
SOUBERIE AV
FIELD
GLADSTONE
LYTTON AVENUE
BROOK
Fearnhill School
HIGH
CHILTERN VIEW
CAMPERS PL
WESTBURY CL
CAMPERS
Westbury School
AV
VIEW
BROADWAY
St Francis College
ROAD
EAST VIEW
Hillbrow
Recreation Ground
AVS
HIGH AVENUE
UNWIN CL
OAK TREE CL
PARKER
SPRING RD
SOLLERSHOTT
LANE
CLOISTERS LAWN
St Christopher School
BARRINGTON
St Thomas More School
SOLLERSHOTT WEST
BROADWAY
Sports School
Ground
The Highfield School
BRIAR PATCH
Playing Field
HITCHIN ROAD
HITCHIN RD
BROADWAY
SPRING RD
LETCHWORTH LANE
MUDDY LA
THE GLADE
MANOR WAY
ALLINGTON LA
PASTURE
PASTURE ROAD
GARTH RD
MANOR RD
MARYS CL
LETCHWORTH ST
THOMANS DAGN
AUBROOK
CROFT
EARLS
HITCHIN
COLLISON CL
ROUNDWOOD CL
COLLISON AVENUE
ARMOUR RSE
GROVELANDS WY
MILLARD
GAINSFORD CR
HARKNESS WY
FRENSHAM DRI
A505
CAMBRIDGE ROAD
ROSEHILL HOSPITAL
Club House
Letchworth Hall Hotel
Golf Course
Tennis Courts
WILLIAN
©Estate Publications
9

LETCHWORTH
7
BALDOCK
A505
Playing Field
Convent
JUBILEE TRADE CENTRE
COTTON BROWN PARK
Works
Supermarket
Electricity Transformer Station
BANK
THE GLADE
THE RISE
ST MARY WY
School
Recreation Ground
Depot
GREENLANE IND. EST.
ASCOT IND. EST.
SHAFTESBURY IND. EST.
Works
Goods Shed
Power Station
WOODSIDE INDUSTRIAL PARK
LETCHWORTH BUSINESS AND RETAIL PARK
BUSINESS CENTRE WEST
BUSINESS CENTRE EAST
ARDEN PRESS WY
Factory
Works WY
PROTEA
Works
AMOR WYS
Leisure Centre
Laundry
Hillshott School
BROUGHTON HILL
Recreation Ground
Sports Ground
Sports Ground
BENNETT CT
HOLMDALE
Garden House Hospice
Football Ground
Woolgrove School
PIXMORE
Pixmore School
Pix Brook
LETCHWORTH
Jackman's Plantation
Radburn School
NEWELLS
PRYOR
QUILLS WAY
OAKHILL
RUNDELLS
MADDLES
WAYSMEET
WAYSBROOK
LORDSHIP LANE
BOWERSHOTT
DENBY
CHATTERTON
BAY WORTH
GOLDEN
IVEL CT
Com. Cen.
Liby.
KYRKEBY
LANNOCK
PARK FIELD
SWANSTAND
A1(M)
BERKELEY
LAWRENCE
WOOLSTON AV
HOWARDS WOOD
HADLEIGH
FLEETWOOD
BELL ACRE
GATE
JARDEN
WHITEWAY
Language Centre
TOWNLEY
Lannock Junior School
HOWARDS GATE
Amb Sta
ASHBOURNE
YARDLEY
VINCENT
MAYLINS
UPRI
A6141
WHITETHORN LANE
Sports Ground
NEWLANDS WAY
BRANDLES ROAD
BLACKMORE
CRABTREE DELL
Playing Field
ALBAN CH
RUDHAM
CHAL FLD
CREAMERY
NORTH ROAD
ROOKES CL
STANE FIELD
OLDEN MEND
MILNE CL
KESTREL WK
ENNISMORE CL
DENTS CLO
Cricket Ground
Normans Farm
A1(M) Junction 9
GREAT
School
FOURACRES
Playing Field
WYRLEY DELL
PEARTREE DELL
NETLEY DELL
LAPWING DELL
FARTHING
DEING DRI
Lordship Farm
Willian
WILLIAN CHURCH RD
ROWLEY CT RD
B197
B197

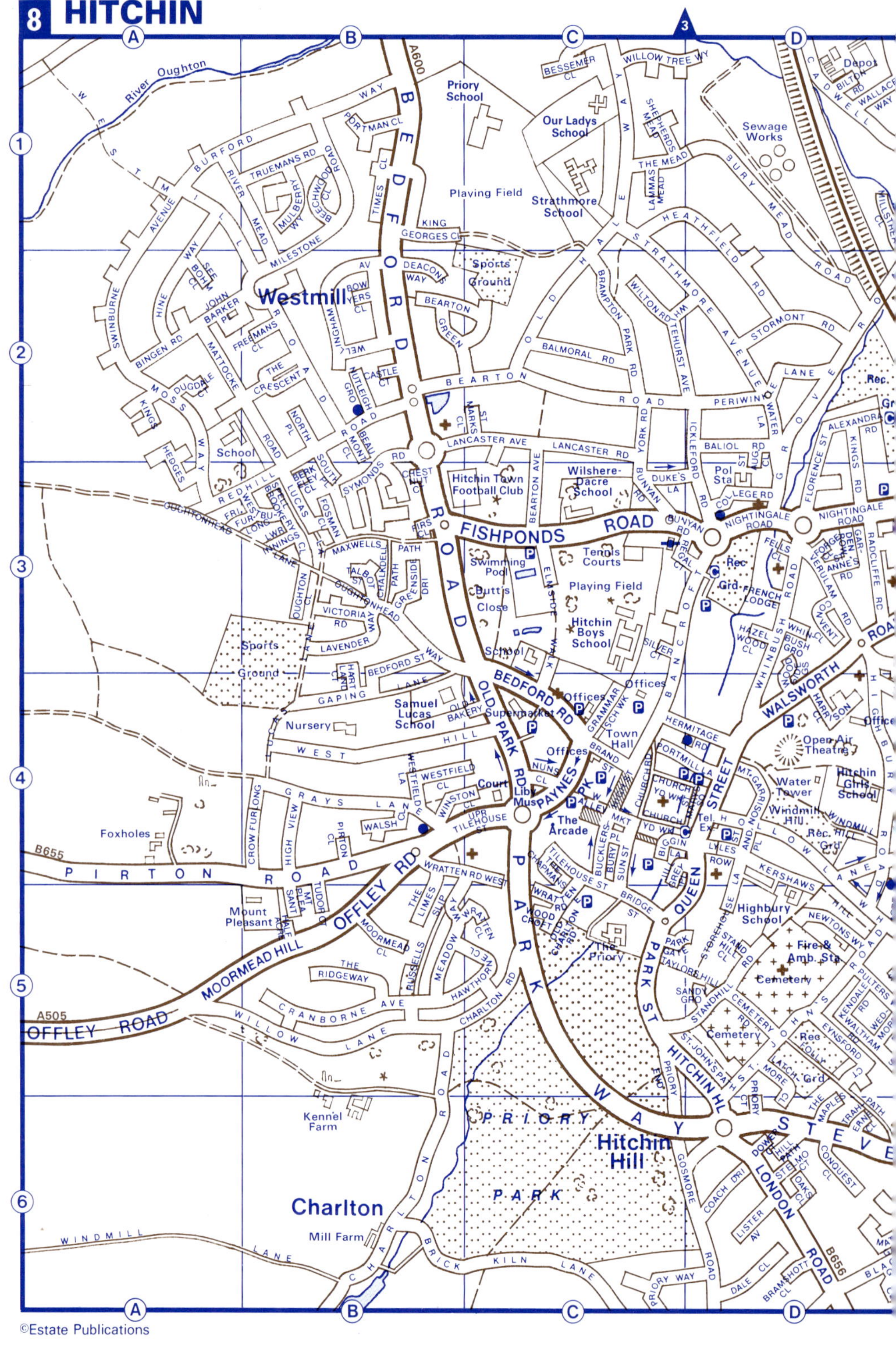
River Oughton
Priory School
Our Ladys School
Willow Tree Wy
Bessemer Cl
Shepherds Mead
Depot
Bilton Rd
Wallace
The Mead
Lammas Mead
Sewage Works
Burford
Way
Portman Cl
Truemans Rd
Beechwood Road
Times Cl
A600
Bedford
Mulberry Wy
Milestone
River Mead
West
Swinburne
Hine
Bohm Cl
John Barker Pl
Freemans Cl
Bow Cl
Bowyers Cl
Welham Cl
Deacons Way
King Georges Cl
Bearton Green
Sports Ground
Strathmore School
Playing Field
Strathmore Avenue
Wilton Rd
Tehurst Av
Brampton Park
Heathfield Rd
Stormont Rd
Periwinkle La
Water
Rec. Gr
Westmill
Avenue
See Way
Bingen Rd
Mattocke Rd
Dugdale Ct
Mos
Kings Way
Hedges
North Pl
The Crescent
Castle Cl
Nutleigh Gro
Beaumont
Road
Bearton
Balmoral Rd
York Rd
Old Road
Ickleford Rd
Duke's La
Bunyan Rd
Baliol Rd
Florence St
Alexandra Rd
Kings Rd
Rd
Nightingale Road
School
Berkeley Cl
South Pl
Symonds Rd
Chalkdell Path
Fosman Cl
Redhill Rd
West Burn
Long
Twinings Cl
Lucas Ct
Maxwells Cl
Firs Cl
Crest Hill Cl
Marks St
St Marks Rd
Lancaster Ave
Lancaster Rd
Bearton Ave
Wilshere-Dacre School
Hitchin Town Football Club
Bunyan Rd
Regal Cl
Pol Sta
College Rd
Fells Cl
Nightingale Road
Radcliffe Rc
Forge End
Verulam Rd
St Annes Rd
Oughtonhead
Oughtonhead Lane
Talbot St
Greenside Dri
Victoria Rd
Road
Fishponds Road
Swimming Pool
Butts Close
Tennis Courts
Playing Field
Hitchin Boys School
Rec Grd
French Lodge
Hazel Wood Cl
Whinbush Gro
Convent
Walsworth Road
Sports Ground
Lavender
Hart La
Bedford St Way
Gaping La
Samuel Lucas School
Old Bakery
School
Silver Ct
Offices
Bedford Rd
Offices
Supermarket
Town Hall
Grammar Sch Wk
Brand St
Back Croft
Hermitage Rd
Portmill La
Open Air Theatre
Hitchin Girls School
Harrison Rd
Whinbush Rd
Nursery
West Hill
Westfield La
Westfield Cl
Court
Lib
Mus
Paynes Pk
Nuns Cl
Offices
Church Yd Wk
Mkt Pl
Church Yd Wk
Tel. Ex.
Water Tower
Windmill HTU
Windmill Hill
Rec. Grd
Foxholes
B655
Crow Furlong
Grays Lane
High View
Pirton Cl
Walsh Cl
Winston Cl
Upr Tilehouse St
The Arcade
Bucklers Pl
Bury
Sun St
Bridge St
Grey Ct
Greyhounds La
Lyles Row
Kershaws Hill
Pirton Road
Mt. Pleasant
Tudor Ct
Offley Rd
The Limes
Slip Way
Wratten Cl
Wratten Rd West
Wood Croft
Charlton Rd
Chapmans Yd
Tilehouse St
Bury St
Park Gate
Taylors Hill
Highbury School
Fire & Amb. Sta
Newtons Wy
Mount Pleasant
Moormead Cl
Russells Cl
Meadow Way
Hawthorn Cl
Hawthorn
Charlton Rd
The Priory
Park St
Standhill Cemetery
Cemetery
Rec. Grd
Eynsford Rd
Waltham
Moormead Hill
The Ridgeway
Cranborne Ave
Willow Lane
Offley Road
A505
Charlton Road
Priory Way
Way
St. John's Path
Hitchin Hill
Priory Rd
Gosmore Rd
Lister Av
London Road
B656
Charlton
Kennel Farm
Mill Farm
Windmill Lane
Brick Kiln Lane
Priory Park
Hitchin Hill
Coach Dri
Stevenage Road

HITCHIN
Walsworth
Purwell
Oakfield
Golf Course
INDUSTRIAL ESTATE
ROSEHILL HOSPITAL
Highover Farm
Highover School
Walsworth Common
Sailor Boy P.H.
Offices
Anchor P.H.
College
Sports Centre
Playing Fields
Purwell Sch
Purwell Mill
Lower Plantation
Upper Plantation
Playing Field
Watercress Beds
The Belt
Mary Exton School
Com Cen
School
Pinehill Hospital
School
NIGHTINGALE ROAD
STA HITCHIN
WALSWORTH RD
TREVOR RD
Whitehill School
Oakfield Farm
Oakhurst
Kingshott School
Grange Farm
Ippollitts Brook
Ash Brook
HITCHIN ROAD
A505
A602
ARCH ROAD
Offices
HILLFIELD AVE
GIRDLE RD
WILBURY WAY
LANE
WOOLGROVE ROAD
DANE
STURGEONS WAY
HIGH
TRISTRAM RD
WEST CL
HIGHOVER
HIGH EAST CL
ORCHARD ROAD
ST FAITHS
GREEN D LA
FRANKLIN GS
HARKNESS
CAMBRIDGE
ARMOUR RISE
GROVELANDS
MILLARD
CHENNELLS
GAINSFORD CR
COLLISON CL
CL
ROUNDWOOD
AVENUE
HARKNESS WY
FRENSHAM DRI
HARKNESS ROAD
STOTFOLD ROAD
QUEENSWOOD DRI
ROAD
CAMBRIDGE ROAD
HAMPDEN ROAD
GRANVILLE RD
MEADOW BANK
COMMON RISE
COMMON RISE
SHARPS WY
COOKS WY
ARNOLD CL
ST MICHAELS
BURNS CL
BYRON CL
BROWNING DRI
CAMPBELL CL
COLERIDGE CLOSE
GIBSON CL
MICHAEL
CHAUCER WAY
DESBORO RD
WIL
PURWELL
River Purwell
MOUNTJOY
BRADLEYS CORNER
WILSHERE CRES
FAIRFIELD WY
KINGSWOOD
AVENUE
MAYLIN CL
BENCHLEY HILL
SANFOINE CL
WILSHERE CRES
MILL LANE
THATCHER'S END
BENSLOW RISE
BENSLOW LANE
THE FINCHES
HITHERSON WAY
CHILTERN RD
WYMONDLEY
SORREL GARTH
SPINNEY CL
HENSLEY CL
BOWMANS AVE
STUART DRI
HALSEY DRIVE
KINGSDOWN
BRAM FIELD
HARDY CL
WEDGEWOOD
KEATS WAY
KIPLING CL
SHELLEY CL
RUSKIN LA
MILTON VW
MASEFIELD
TENNYSON AVE
TALISMAN
CUB STIRLING CL
STURT WY
ROCK ST
LINTEN CL
BROOKVIEW
UPLANDS RD
MANTON RD
ASTON
NINE SPRINGS WAY
SPRINGS AVE
OAKFIELD AV
LINDSAY AVE
MANOR CRES
BROADMEAD
POPLAR CL
WHITEHILL CL
WESTWOOD
WILLOUGHBY WAY
THE ASPENS
KARD WELL CL
ORLANDO CL
WALNUT CL
THE BEECHES
MAY
WILLOWS
THE PADDOCK
MOWBRAY GS
BLACKHORSE CL
LANGBRIDGE
ROAD

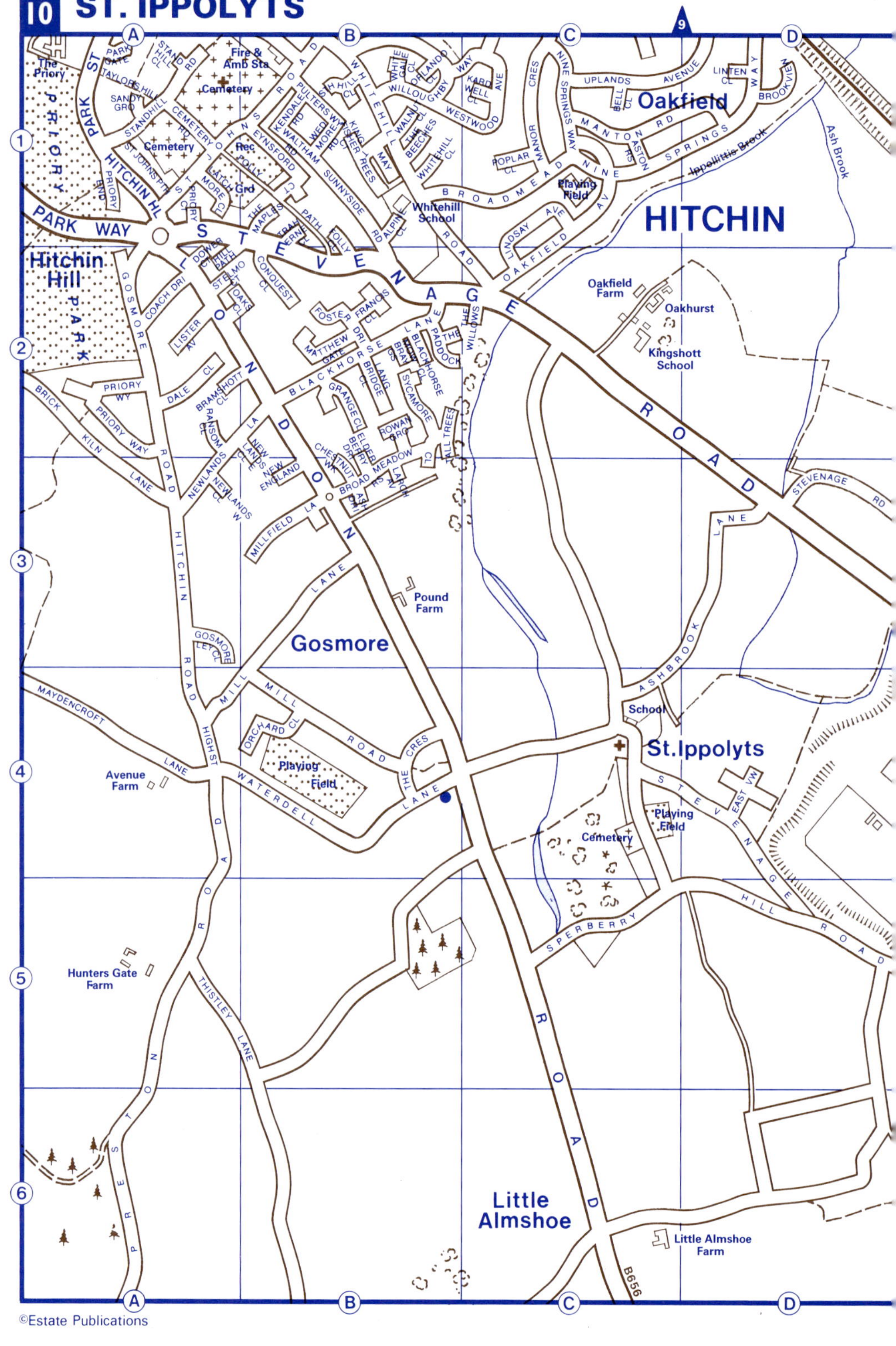
The Priory
Hitchin Hill
PRIORY PARK
PARK WAY
PARK ST
HITCHIN HL
PRIORY END
ST JOHNS PTH
PARK GATE
TAYLORS HILL
SANDY GRO
STANDHILL
STANDHILL RD
CEMETERY O
Cemetery
Cemetery
Fire & Amb Sta
Rec
LATCH Grd
FOLLY
MORE CL
PRIORY
THE MAPLES
DOWER
HILL PATH
STELMO
OAKS
CONQUEST CL
COACH DRI
GOSMORE
LISTER AV
DALE CL
BRAMSHOTT CL
RANSOM CL
PRIORY WY
PRIORY WAY
BRICK KILN LANE
HITCHIN ROAD
NEWLANDS CL
NEWLANDS CL W
MILLFIELD LA
NEW LANES
NEW ENGLAND
MILL LANE
LONDON LANE
MATTHEW GATE
FOSTER DRI
FRANCIS CL
GRANGE CL
BLACKHORSE LANE
CHESTNUT WK
BROAD MEADOW
ASH
BLACKHORSE LANE
BRAY CL
SYCAMORE
ELDERBERRY
ROWAN GRO
BERRY CL
LARCH
TALL TREES
THE WILLOWS
THE PADDOCK
KENDALLS FLD
EYNSFORD
WALTHAM RD
WED
PULTERS WAY
HILL CL
SUNNYSIDE
ALPINE
FOLLY
SUNNYSIDE RD
STEVENAGE ROAD
WHITEHILL CL
KING REES
WALNUT CL
BEECHES
WHITEHILL CL
WHITEHILL CL
WHITE GATE
ORLANDO CL
WILLOUGHBY WAY
WESTWOOD
KARD CL
WELL
BROADMEAD
POPLAR CL
LINDSAY AVE
OAKFIELD
AVE
NINE SPRINGS WAY
MANOR CRES
MANTON RD
ASTON RS
NINE SPRINGS AV
UPLANDS
BELL
AVENUE
LINTEN CL
BROOKVIEW
WAY
Oakfield
Playing Field
Whitehill School
HITCHIN
Ash Brook
Ippollittle Brook
Oakfield Farm
Oakhurst
Kingshott School
ROAD
STEVENAGE RD
ASHBROOK LANE
Pound Farm
Gosmore
MAYDENCROFT LANE
HIGH ST
ORCHARD CL
WATERDELL
Playing Field
GOSMORE LETCH CL
Avenue Farm
THE CRES
LANE
MILL CL
MILL ROAD
School
St.Ippolyts
Playing Field
Cemetery
STEVENAGE ROAD
EAST VW
SPERBERRY
STEVENAGE HILL ROAD
Hunters Gate Farm
THISTLEY LANE
PRESTON ROAD
B656
Little Almshoe
Little Almshoe Farm

E F G H
HITCHIN ROAD
GRAVELEY ROAD
Playing Field
Grange Farm
Great Wymondley
GRAVELEY LANE
1
STEVENAGE ROAD
PRIORY LANE
2
Remains of Priory (Augustinian)
GRIMSTONE RD
SICCUT ROAD
GRIMSTONE RD
School
PRIORY VW
ELMS CL
WATERLOW MS
STEVENAGE ROAD
BLADON CL
3
Blakemore Hotel
Little Wymondley
TOWER CL
CHURCH PATH
ROAD
12
A1(M) Junction 8
BLAKEMORE END ROAD
Cricket Ground
CHANTRY LA
4
Wymondley Transforming Station
OLD CHANTRY LA
Depot
STEVENAGE ROAD
Bury Wood
CHANTRY ROAD
Margaret's Wood
HITCHIN RD
Supermarket
Titmore Green
Todd's Green
A1(M)
INGLESIDE DRI
BARON LANE
HERNE RD
CAISTER AV
FISHERS GREEN
GORLESTON CL
5
Redcoats Farm
Titmore Farm
KESSINGLAND
ALDE
BURGH CL
SHERINGHAM RD
MUNDESLEY CL
BAWDSEY CL
CORTON CL
Fishers Green
FISHERS GRN RD
Lucas's Wood
FISHERS GREEN
BERWICK CL
CLOVELLY WAY
FISHERS GRN
SYMONDS RD
FISHERS GRN RD
6
E F G H

12 GRAVELEY
A
B
C
D
1
2
3
11
4
5
6
B197
The Beeches
Graveley Hall Farm
Ledge Side Plantation
GRAVELEY LANE
OAK LA
CHURCH LANE
HIGH ST
COMMON
ASHWELL
ASHWELL CL
POND SIDE
GRINDERS END
School
Graveley
Cricket Ground
A1(M)
Ten Acre Plantation
Gorsedell Plantation
GRAVELEY ROAD
A1(M) Junction 8
NORTH ROAD
Sports Ground
Depot
Supermarket
HITCHIN ROAD
TATES WAY
COREYS
LISTER HOSPITAL
CP
Cuckoo Wood
GRANBY
DALTRY RD
CL
UNDERWOOD RD
CHOULER CL
TURNER CL
WYMBLES
BRITTEN
THURLOW CL
ARNOLD
ROOKS NEST FARM BARNS
GLOUCESTER
CASTER
ASHBY
ST ALBANS LINK
WAY
NOR
INGLESIDE
BARON
HERNE RD
CHAPMAN DRIVE
ANSELL DRI
MILL LANE
WHITNEY WOOD
WALLED GARDEN
WIGGINS WK
THE TOD
WOOD FIELD RD
CHANCELLORS ROAD
FOSTER
BOSWELL
GS
CHANCELLORS ROAD
NEW BURY
WILSON CL
MORGAN CL
MATT CL
EWS CL
Cemetery
GUILD CL
ST ALBANS ROAD
DRI
GREAT
CANTERBURY WAY
YORK WAY
FISHERS GREEN LANE
MURL DESLEY CL
SHERINGHAM RD
BAWDSEY
CORTON CL
School
TUDOR CL
BURY MEAD
RECTORY CROFT
THE CLOSE
NICHOLAS CL
CHESTNUT CL
The Bury
St. Nicholas's
WESTON
TRAFFORD CL
WESTON RD
School
BADER
STATIN
TRUMPER
GRACE
TRENT CL
HEADINGLEY CL
TRUMPER RD
YORK WAY
FISHERS GRN
FISHERS GRN RD
GUNNELS WOOD RD
School
WHITNEY DRIVE
RECTORY
BURY MEAD
MARTINS ROAD
Football Ground
THE AVENUE
Playing Field
15
©Estate Publications

Stonesley Wood
Claypits Wood
WESTON ROAD
Friend's Green Farm
Warrensgreen Wood
Harbourclose Wood
Tilekiln Farm
Riding School
Tilekiln Wood
Longdell Wood
Round Wood
New Spring
Nine Acre Wood
THE CHILTERNS
Brooches Wood
HUMBER CT
KENMARE CL
AVENUE RICCAT LA
BOTANY BAY LANE
SWALE CL
BRAY DRI
WINDRUSH CL
GREAT ASHBY WAY
BLACKDOWN CL
GREAT ASHBY WAY
CLEVELAND WAY
RYDERS HILL
MT KEEN
QUANTOCK CL
WENSUM RD
KENT
DOVE DRI
CALDER WAY
WAY
YERWELL DRI
Nursery
Com Cen
PENTLAND RD
FAIRFIELD
GRASMERE WAY
Park Plantation
SEVERN
TEES
WYE WAY
ORWELL
TAMAR CL
WANSBECK CL
GREAT ASHBY
FOYLE
GT ASHBY WY
NEAGH CL
LOMOND CL
LOWES CL
MANCHESTER CL
OLD ASHBY
BOURNE
St. Nicholas Park
WAY
Hangbois Wood
SERPENTINE
NEWCASTLE CL
GREAT CLOSE RD
WESTON RD
SALISBURY RD
LINCOLN RD
WHITWORTH RD
WEDGE WOOD CT
GREAT ASHBY WAY
WINDERMERE
ST DAVIDS CL
ASHBY WAY
WINCHESTER CL
BEVERLEY RD
Wellfield
DENLITE
BOULTON RD
EASTMAN WAY
PARSONS
THIRLMERE
Recreation Ground
EXETER CL
Depot
Wedgewood Wood
Depot
PIN GREEN INDUSTRIAL AREA
District Park
STEVENAGE
PILGRIMS WAY
SOUTH WARK CL
ELY
WEDGEWOOD
CARTWRIGHT
Warehouse
Nature Reserve
RIPON ROAD
COVENTRY CL
NORWICH CL
WEDGEWOOD ROAD
BOX WOOD
St. Nicholas
CANTERBURY ROAD
CHESTER RD
ASCOT CRES
ASCOT CRES
Martin's Wood
School
MARTINS ROAD
WAY
GRESLEY WAY
YORK
DURHAM ROAD
MARTINS WAY
SEFTON ROAD
Sch
LINGFIELD ROAD
GORDIAN
TRAJAN
VALERIAN
WISDEN ROAD
JESSOP ROAD
BRADMAN WY
VERITY WAY
MILDMAY
DERBY WAY
CRES
SANDOWN ROAD
WETHERBY CL
MINERVA CL
JULIA GATE
NEPTUNE WY
Schools
Pin Green
VARDON ROAD
JESSOP ROAD
CHEPSTOW CL
DONCASTER CL
AYR CL
AYR CL
APOLLO WY
PACATIAN WY
AUGUSTUS GATE
JUPITER GT
WISDEN ROAD

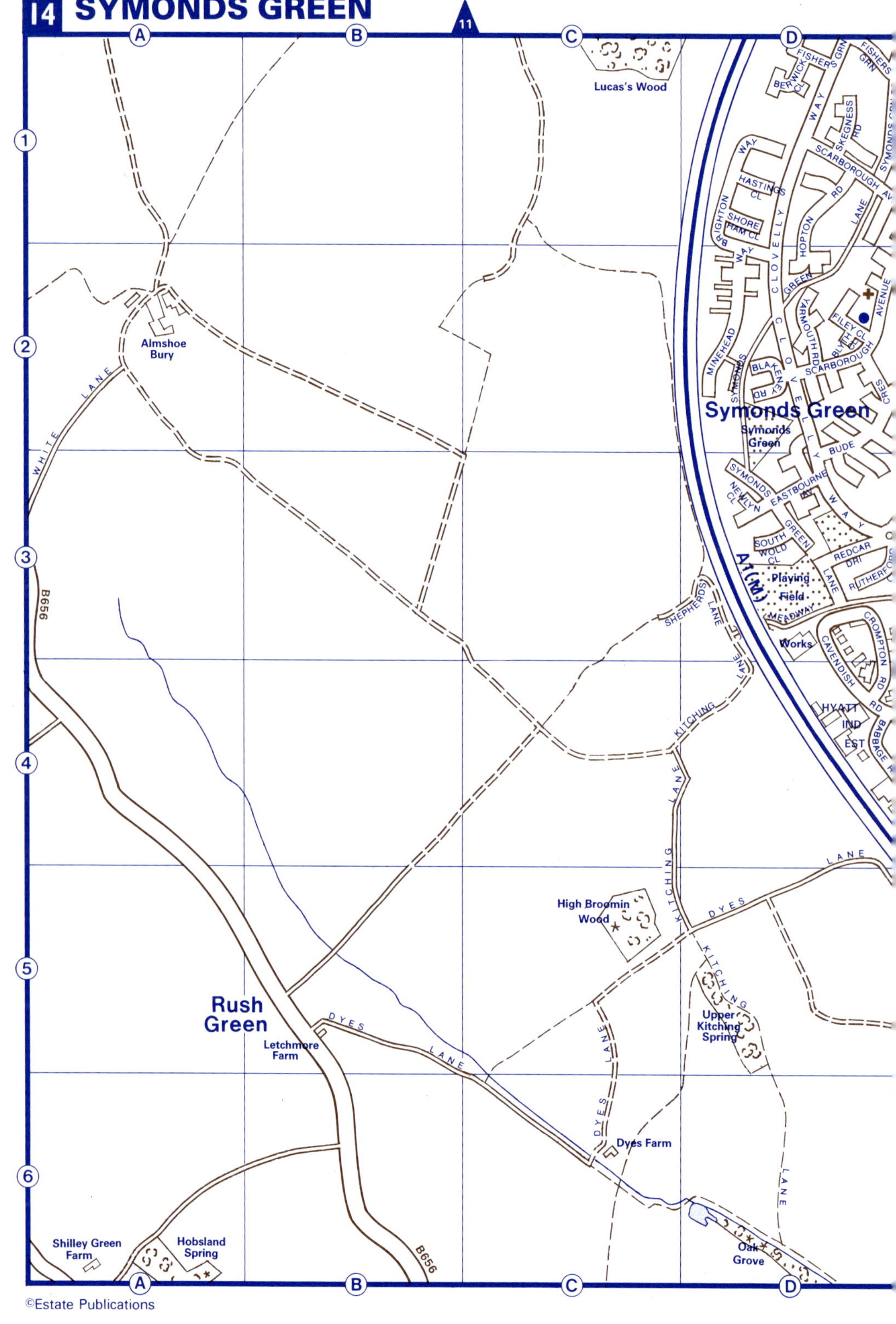
11
A B C D
1
2
3
4
5
6
Lucas's Wood
FISHERS GRN
FISHERS GRN
BERWICK CL
WAY
SKEGNESS
SCARBOROUGH AV
HASTINGS CL
SHORE HAM CL
BRIGHTON
WAY
MINEHEAD
SYMONDS
NEWLYN CL
SOUTH WOLD CL
CLOVELLY GREEN
HOPTON CL
YARMOUTH RD
FILEY CL
BLYTH CL
SCARBOROUGH
BLAKENEY RD
SYMONDS GREEN RD
AVENUE
CRES
Symonds Green
Symonds Green
EASTBOURNE WAY
BUDE WAY
REDCAR
RUTHERFORD
A1(M)
SHEPHERDS
SQ LANE
KITCHING LANE
Playing Field
MEADWAY
Works
CAVENDISH RD
CROMPTON RD
BABBAGE
HYATT IND EST
WHITE LANE
Almshoe Bury
B656
High Broomin Wood
KITCHING LANE
DYES LANE
Upper Kitching Spring
KITCHING LANE
Rush Green
Letchmore Farm
DYES LANE
DYES LANE
Dyes Farm
B656
Shilley Green Farm
Hobsland Spring
Oak Grove

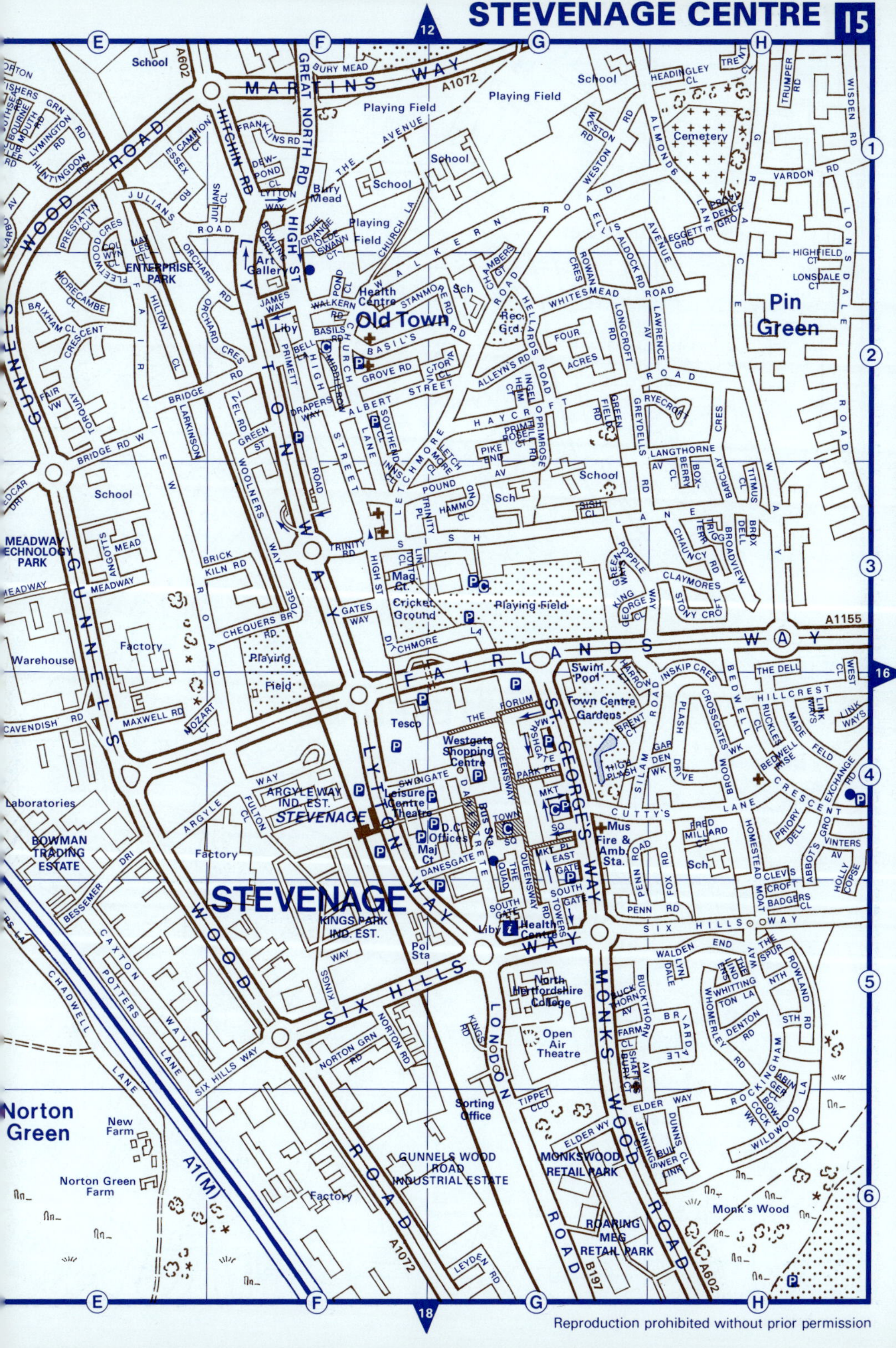
STEVENAGE CENTRE
MARTINS WAY
GREAT NORTH ROAD
BURY MEAD
A1072
Playing Field
Playing Field
School
HEADINGLEY CL
TRUMPER
WISDEN RD
School
A602
HITCHIN RD
WOOD ROAD
GUNNELS
THE AVENUE
WESTON RD
CEMETERY
VARDON RD
LONSDALE ROAD
Pin Green
Enterprise Park
Art Gallery
HIGH ST
LYTTON WAY
Old Town
Health Centre
ST BASIL'S
GROVE RD
STREET
WALKERN ROAD
HELLARDS ROAD
WHITESMEAD RD
LAWRENCE
AVENUE
LEGGETT DRIVE
HIGHFIELD CT
LONSDALE CT
Rec. Grd.
FOUR ACRES
GREEN FIELDS
LANGTHORNE AV
BOXBERRY
BARCLAY
TITMUS CL
BROADVIEW
Meadway Technology Park
MEADWAY
School
BRICK KILN RD
CHEQUERS BRIDGE RD
ALBERT STREET
SOUTHEND
LETCHMORE
TRINITY RD
HAYCROFT
PRIMROSE RD
School
KING GEORGE'S WAY
POPPLE WAY
CHAUNCY
CLAYMORES
STONY CROFT
A1155
Warehouse
Factory
Playing Field
GATES WAY
DITCHMORE
HIGH ST
TRINITY RD
Magistrates Court
Cricket Ground
Playing Field
Swim Pool
Town Centre Gardens
HIGH PLASH
CROSSGATES
BEDWELL
THE DELL
HILLCREST
WEST CL
LINK WAYS
MADE FELD
CAVENDISH RD
MAXWELL RD
MOZART CT
FAIRLANDS WAY
Tesco
THE FORUM
Westgate Shopping Centre
PARK PLACE
QUEENSWAY
BRENT CT
GARDEN WK
PLASH DRIVE
BEDWELL CRESCENT
RUCKLES
EXCHANGE RD
Laboratories
ARGYLE WAY IND. EST.
STEVENAGE
Leisure Centre
SWINGATE
FULTON CL
ARGYLE
Factory
D.C. Offices
Major Court
BUS STATION
TOWN SQUARE
THE QUADRANT
ST GEORGE'S WAY
MARKET
SOUTHGATE
EASTGATE
Museum
Fire & Amb. Sta.
FRED MILLARD
Sch
PRIORY DELL
ABBOT'S GROVE
VINTERS AV
HOLLY COPSE
BOWMAN TRADING ESTATE
BESSEMER DRIVE
WOOD
STEVENAGE
KINGS PARK IND. EST.
KINGS WAY
DANESGATE
SOUTHGATE
TOWERS
Health Centre
PENN ROAD
FOX RD
CLEVIS CROFT
BADGERS CL
MOAT
SIX HILLS WAY
CHADWELL LANE
POTTERS WAY
CAXTON WAY
SIX HILLS WAY
SIX HILLS WAY
NORTON GRN
NORTON RD
LONDON ROAD
North Hertfordshire College
Open Air Theatre
BUCKTHORN AV
WHITTINGTON LA
WHOMERLEY RD
DENTON RD
WALDEN END
THE SPUR
ROWLAND RD
ROCKINGHAM
WILDWOOD
Norton Green
New Farm
Norton Green Farm
A1(M)
Factory
A1072
Sorting Office
TIPPET CLO
GUNNELS WOOD ROAD INDUSTRIAL ESTATE
MONKSWOOD RETAIL PARK
MONKS WOOD ROAD
ELDER WAY
JENNINGS
DUNNS CL
Monk's Wood
A602
LEYDEN RD
B197
ROARING MEG RETAIL PARK
Reproduction prohibited without prior permission

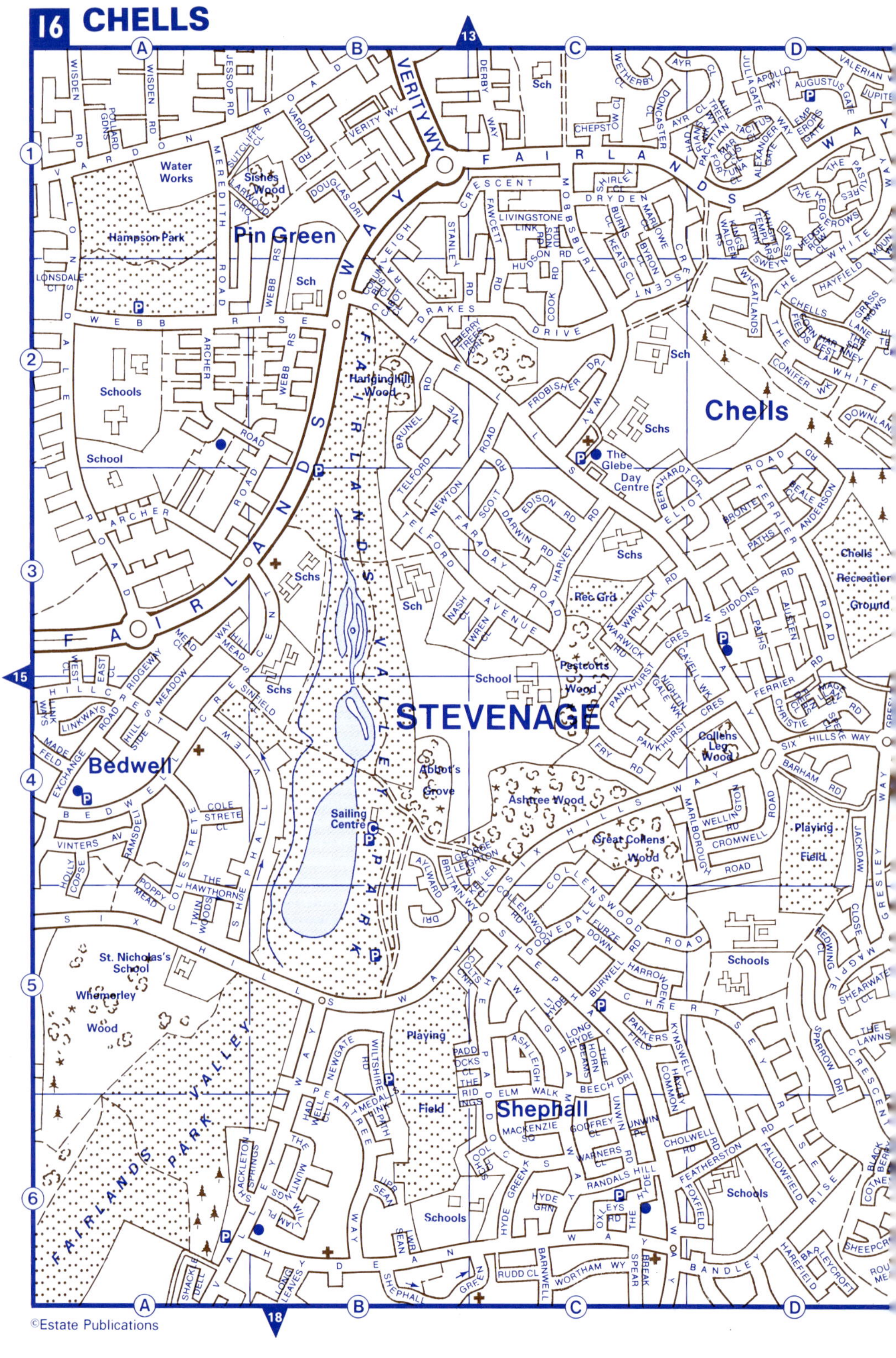
CHELLS
STEVENAGE
Pin Green
Bedwell
Shephall
Water Works
Hampson Park
Sishes Wood
Hanging Hill Wood
Schools
School
The Glebe Day Centre
Chells Recreation Ground
Rec Grd
Pescotts Wood
Abbot's Grove
Ashtree Wood
Great Collens Wood
Collens Leg Wood
Sailing Centre
St. Nicholas's School
Whomerley Wood
Playing Field
Playing Field
Schools
Fairlands Valley Park
Verity Wy
Fairlands Way
Fairlands Road
Jessop Rd
Wisden Rd
Wisden Rd
Pollard Rd
Meredith Road
Sutcliffe Cl
Larwood Gro
Vardon Rd
Douglas Dri
Webb Rise
Archer Road
Archer Road
Webb Rise
Lonsdale Cl
Derby Way
Crescent
Fawcett
Livingstone Link
Stanley Rd
Hudson Rd
Cook Rd
Drakes Drive
Brunel
Telford Rd
Telford Road
Newton Rd
Scott Rd
Faraday Road
Darwin Rd
Edison Rd
Harvey
Nash Cl
Wren Cl
Avenue
Frobisher Dri
Wetherby
Chepstow
Doncaster
Ayr Cl
Shirley Rd
Dryden
Burns
Keats Cl
Byron
Marlowe
Mobbsbury Way
Bernhardt Cr
Eliot Rd
Warwick Rd
Warwick Rd
Pankhurst
Nightingale Wk
Cavell Wk
Siddons Rd
Ferrier Paths
Austen Rd
Anderson Road
Bronte
Beale
Ferrier Road
Christie
Fry Rd
Pankhurst Cres
Six Hills Way
Barham Rd
Wellington Rd
Marlborough Road
Cromwell Road
Collenswood Road
Furze Down
Burwell
Harrowdene
Chertsey
Kymswell Rd
Featherston Rd
Foxfield
Fallowfield
Valley Park
Hackleton
Long Springs
The Muntings
Hadley Wall
Peartree Way
Newgate
Wiltshire
Medalls Link Path
The Ridings
Shephall Way
Aylward
Brittain Wy
Keller Cl
George Leighton Ct
Colts Cnr
Paddocks Cl
Elm Walk
Ashleigh
Beech Dri
Long Hyde
The Horn
The Beams
Mackenzie Sq
Godfrey Cl
Warners End
Unwin Rd
Cholwell Rd
Randals Hill
Oxleys Rd
Hyde Grn
Break Spear
Bandley
Harefield
Barleycroft
Sheepcot
Apollo Wy
Augustus Gate
Valerian
Jupiter
Emperors Gate
Alexander Way
Tacitus Cl
Fortuna
Knights Templars Grn
The Hedgerows
Chells Lane
Conifer Wk
Downlands
Sparrow Dri
The Lawns
Shearwater
Redwing Cl
Magpie
Jackdaw
Gresley Way
P

STEVENAGE
ROAD
B1037
Walkern
THE MALTINGS
FINCHES
Sch
WRIGHTS MDW
GREENWAY
Playing Field
GRESLEY WAY
BOXFIELD GDN
UPLANDS
SHELFANDS
CHALKDOWN WAY
AVE
BEANE
BEANE WK
BEANE RD
VALLEY WAY
LANTERNS LA
Poultry Farm
SHEAFGREEN LA
LONG LANE
HOLDERS LANE
New Wood
BENINGTON ROAD
BENINGTON ROAD
River Beane
White Farm
Lord's Farm
Aston End
WATERCRESS CL
WALNUT TREE CL
MILESTONE CL
EDMONDS CL
CARTERS CL
PARISHES MEAD
COOPERS CL
TATLERS
DRIVE
LIME CL
GRESLEY
LANE
SHORT LANE
ASTON END ROAD
Haily Park Wood
Hubbert's Grove
HIGH
WOOD
Aston End Brook
Supermarket
Poplars
MAGPIE CRES
SKYLARK CNR
FIELDFARE
MINSDEN ROAD
LAPWING
MEAD ROAD
WAY
ARUNDEL CL
Sch
BROOKFIELD LANE
WALKERN ROAD

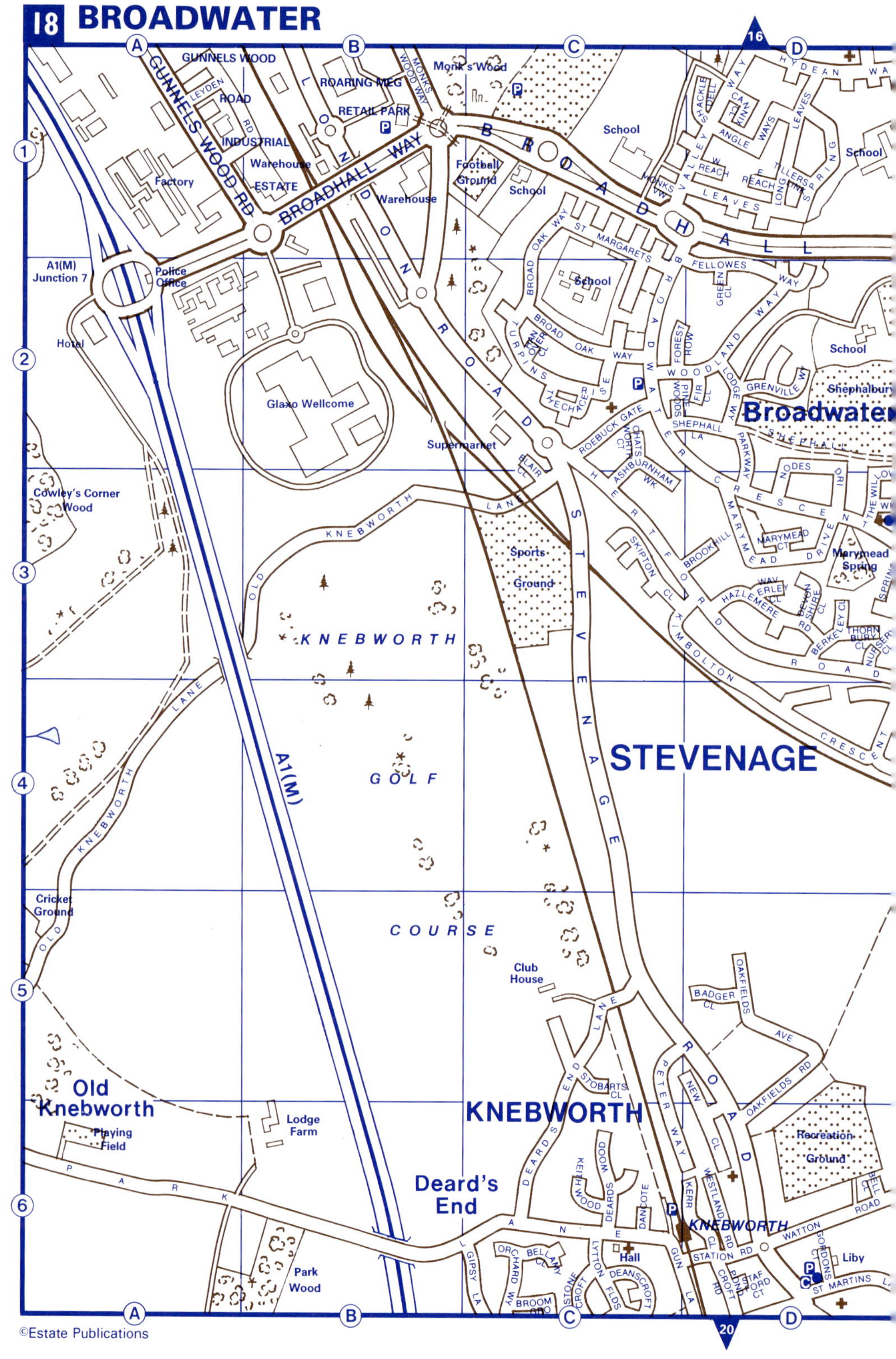
16
GUNNELS WOOD
Monk's Wood
LEYDEN
ROARING MEG
GUNNELS WOOD ROAD
RETAIL PARK
School
MONKS WOOD WAY
School
INDUSTRIAL
Warehouse
Football Ground
BROADHALL WAY
VALLEY SHACKLE WAY
HYDEAN WAY
FACTORY
ESTATE
School
CANNIX
ANGLE
TILLERS
LONGSPRING
WAY REACH
Warehouse
BROAD OAK WAY
ST MARGARETS
GREEN CL
FELLOWES
W REACH
LEAVES
School
School
A1(M) Junction 7
Police Office
BROAD OAK WAY
ROAD
FOREST ROW
WAY
BROADHALL
Hotel
School
TURPINS
RISE
THE CHACE
WOODLAND WY
FIR
LODGE WY
GRENVILLE WY
Shephalbury
Glaxo Wellcome
WATER
MARYMEAD
PARKWAY
SHEPHALL
Broadwater
Supermarket
BLAIR CL
ROEBUCK GATE
CHATSWORTH CT
ASHBURNHAM WK
SKIPTON CL
BROOKHILL CL
MARYMEAD CT
NODES DRI
THE WILLO
Cowley's Corner Wood
LANE
KNEBWORTH
Sports Ground
HERTFORD
HAZLEMERE
KIMBOLTON
MARYMEAD
Marymead Spring
WAV
BELTON RD
ERLEY CL
DEVONSHIRE CL
BERKELEY CL
THORNBURY CL
NURSERY
ROAD
OLD
KNEBWORTH
STEVENAGE
CRESCENT
GOLF
A1(M)
STEVENAGE
KNEBWORTH LANE
COURSE
Cricket Ground
OLD
Club House
BADGER CL
OAKFIELDS CL
AVE
OAKFIELDS RD
Old Knebworth
LANE
PETER WAY
NEW ROAD
Playing Field
DEARDS END
STOBARTS CL
Recreation Ground
PARK
Lodge Farm
KNEBWORTH
KEITHWOOD
DEARDS WOOD
DANCOTE
KERR CL
WESTLAND RD
BELL ROAD
Deard's End
STONE CROFT
NEW ROAD
STATION RD
GUN LA
STAFFORD CT
KNEBWORTH
WATTON RD
GORDONS
Liby
GIPSY LA
ORCHARD WY
BELLAMY CL
LYTTON FIELDS
DEANSCROFT
Hall
P
BROOM RD
ST MARTINS L
Park Wood
20

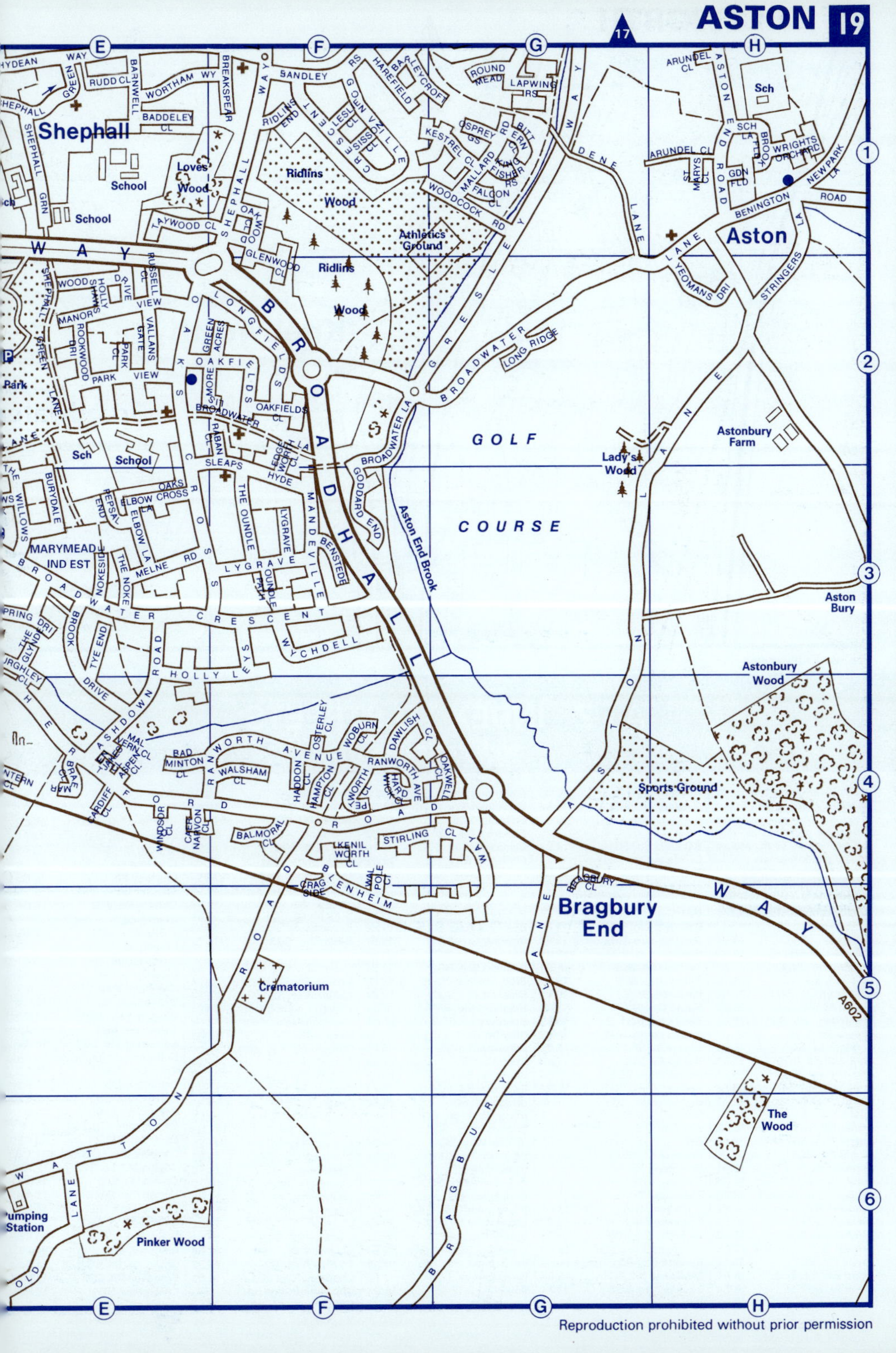

ASTON
19
17
Shephall
HYDEAN WAY
GREEN WAY
RUDD CL
BARNWELL
WORTHAM WY
BREAKSPEAR
SANDLEY
WAY
RIDLINS END
GRESLEY CRESCENT
GOUNVILLE CL
SISSON CL
RS
HAREFIELD
BARLEYCROFT
ROUND MEAD
LAPWING
RS
ARUNDEL CL
Sch
SHEPHALL
BADDELEY CL
Loves Wood
Ridlins
Wood
KESTREL CL
OSPREY GS
RD
BITTERN
KING FISHER
MALLARD
WOODCOCK RD
FALCON
DENE LANE
ARUNDEL CL
SCH LA
MARYS CL
ST
ASTON END ROAD
GDN FLD
BROOK
WRIGHTS ORCHARD
NEW PARK
Aston
School
School
LAYWOOD CL
OAKWOOD
SHEPHALL
GLENWOOD CL
Ridlins
Wood
Athletics Ground
YEOMANS DRI
BENINGTON
ROAD
STRINGERS LA
1
W A Y
SHEPHALL GREEN LANE
WOOD SHAWS
HOLLY SHAWS
MANOR DRIVE
DRIVE
RUSSELL
GATE
VALLANS CL
LONGFIELDS
GREEN ACRES
OAKS
BROADWATER
B R O A D W A T E R
LONG RIDGE
2
P
Park
ROOKWOOD DRI
PARK VIEW
MORE
OAKFIELDS
OAKFIELDS CL
BROADWATER LA
GODDARD END
GOLF
Astonbury Farm
THE
THE WILLOWS
BURYDALE
Sch
School
OAKS
EGERTON WOOD
RABAN
SLEAPS
HYDE
BENSTEDE
Lady's Wood
LANE
Astonbury Wood
MARYMEAD IND EST
REPSAL
ELBOW CROSS
ELBOW LA
THE NOKE
MELNE RD
THE OUNDLE
LYGRAVE
LYGRAVE
OUNDLE
MANDEVILLE
Aston End Brook
C O U R S E
ASTON
3
BROADWATER
BROOK
SPRING DRI
DIXIE
NOKESIDE
CROSS
ROAD
HOLLY LEYS
LEYS
CRESCENT
WYCHDELL
Aston Bury
KEIGHLEY CL
TYE END
DRIVE
ASHDOWN
OSTERLEY CL
WOBURN CL
DAWLISH CL
OAKWELL
Astonbury Wood
4
LANTERN CL
BRAE
MALVERN CL
ASPEN CL
BAD MINTON CL
RANWORTH
HADDON
WALSHAM CL
HAMPTON
PETWORTH
RANWORTH AVE
HARDWICK
LANE
Sports Ground
CARDIFF
NARVON CL
WINDSOR CL
CHEPSTOW
BALMORAL CL
KENILWORTH CL
STIRLING CL
WALPOLE
WAY
BRAGBURY CL
W A Y
CRAG SIDE
BLENHEIM
Bragbury End
A602
5
Crematorium
BRAGBURY LANE
WATTON
LANE
OLD
W
Pumping Station
The Wood
6
Pinker Wood
Reproduction prohibited without prior permission
E
F
G
H

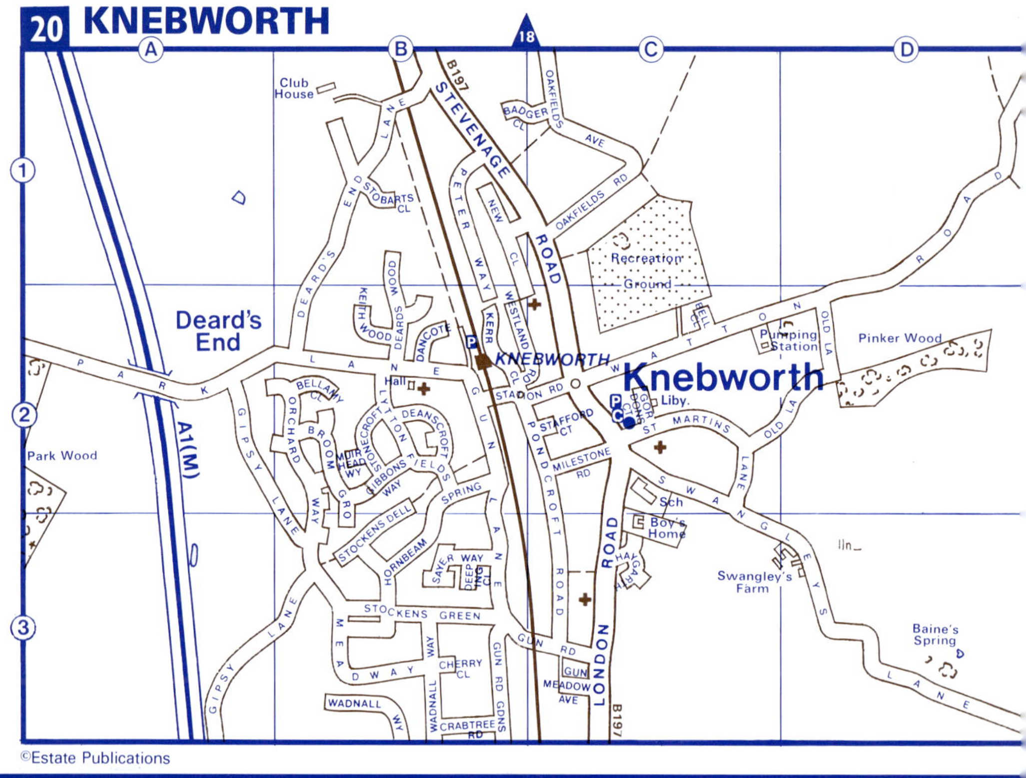

A - Z INDEX TO STREETS
with Postcodes

The Index includes some names for which there is insufficient space on the maps. These names are preceded by an * and are followed by the nearest adjoining thoroughfare.

STEVENAGE

Abbots Gro. SG1	15 H4
Abinger Clo. SG1	15 H5
Aintree Way. SG1	16 D1
Albert St. SG1	15 F2
Aldeburgh Clo. SG1	11 H6
Aldock Rd. SG1	15 G1
Alexander Gate. SG1	16 D1
Alleyns Rd. SG1	15 G2
Almonds La. SG1	15 H1
Anderson Rd. SG1	16 D3
Angle Ways. SG1	18 D1
Angotts Mead. SG1	15 E3
Ansell Ct. SG1	12 A5
Apollo Way. SG2	16 D1
Archer Rd. SG1	16 A2
Argyle Way. SG1	15 E4
Arnold Clo. SG1	12 C5
Arundel Clo. SG1	19 H1
Ascot Cres. SG1	13 G5
Ashburnham Wk. SG1	18 C3
Ashdown Rd. SG1	19 E4
Ashleigh. SG1	16 C5
Ashwell Clo. SG4	12 A3
Ashwell Common. SG4	12 A3
Aspen Clo. SG2	19 E4
Aston End Rd. SG2	19 H1
Aston La. SG2	19 G4
Augustus Gate. SG2	13 H6

Austen Paths. SG2	16 D3
Aylward Dri. SG2	16 B4
Ayr Clo. SG1	16 C1
Babbage Rd. SG1	14 D4
Baddeley Clo. SG2	19 E1
Bader Clo. SG1	12 D6
Badger Clo. SG3	20 C1
Badgers Clo. SG1	15 H5
Badminton Clo. SG2	19 E4
Balmoral Clo. SG2	19 F4
Bandley Rise. SG2	19 F1
Barclay Cres. SG1	15 H3
Barham Rd. SG2	16 D4
Barleycroft. SG2	19 F1
Barnwell. SG2	19 E1
Baron Ct. SG1	12 A5
Basil's Rd. SG1	15 F2
Bawdsey Clo. SG1	12 A6
Beale Clo. SG2	16 D3
Beane Av. SG2	17 E2
Beane Walk. SG2	17 E3
Bedwell Cres. SG1	15 H4
Bedwell Rise. SG1	15 H4
Beech Dri. SG2	16 C5
Bell Clo. SG3	20 C2
Bell La. SG1	15 F2
Bellamy Clo. SG3	20 B2
Benington Rd, Aston. SG2	19 H1
Benington Rd, Walkern. SG2	17 H2
Benstede. SG2	19 F3
Berkeley Clo. SG2	18 D3
Bernhardt Cres. SG2	16 C3
Berwick Clo. SG1	11 H6
Bessemer Dri. SG1	15 E5
Beverley Rd. SG1	13 F4
Bittern Clo. SG2	19 G1

Blackberry Mead. SG2	16 D6
Blackdown Clo. SG1	13 G3
Blair Clo. SG2	18 C2
Blakeney Rd. SG1	14 D2
Blenheim Way. SG2	19 F4
Blyth Clo. SG1	14 D2
Boswell Gdns. SG1	12 C5
Botany Bay La. SG1	13 F3
Boulton Rd. SG1	13 G4
Bournemouth Rd. SG1	15 E1
Bowcock Walk. SG1	15 H6
Bowling Grn. SG1	15 F1
Boxberry Clo. SG1	15 H3
Boxfield Grn. SG2	17 E1
Bradman Way. SG1	13 F6
Braemar Clo. SG2	19 E4
Bragbury Clo. SG2	19 G4
Bragbury La. SG2	19 G6
Bray Dri. SG1	13 F3
Breakspear. SG2	19 F1
Brent Ct. SG1	15 G4
Briardale. SG1	15 H5
Brick Kiln Rd. SG1	15 F3
Bridge Rd. SG1	15 E2
Bridge Rd West. SG1	15 E2
Brighton Way. SG1	14 D1
Brittain Way. SG2	16 B4
Brixham Clo. SG1	15 E2
Broad Oak Way. SG2	18 C2
Broadhall Way. SG2	18 B1
Broadview. SG1	15 H3
Broadwater Cres. SG2	18 C2
Broadwater La. SG2	19 F2
Bronte Paths. SG2	16 D3
Brook Dri. SG2	19 E3
Brook Field. SG2	19 H1
Brookfield La. SG2	17 F6
Brookhill. SG2	18 D3
Broom Gro. SG3	20 B2

Broom Walk. SG1	15 H4
Brox Dell. SG1	15 H3
Brunel Rd. SG2	16 B2
Buckthorn Av. SG1	15 G5
Bude Cres. SG1	14 D2
Bulwer Link. SG1	15 H6
Burghley Ct. SG2	19 E3
Burns Clo. SG2	16 C1
Burwell Rd. SG2	16 C5
Bury Mead. SG1	12 B6
Burydale. SG2	19 E3
Byron Clo. SG2	16 C2
Cabot Clo. SG2	16 B2
Caernarvon Clo. SG2	19 E4
Calder Way. SG1	13 E4
Campion Ct. SG1	15 E1
Campkin Mead. SG2	17 E6
Cannix Clo. SG2	18 D1
Canterbury Way. SG1	12 D6
Cardiff Clo. SG2	19 E4
Carters Clo. SG2	17 E5
Cartwright Rd. SG1	13 G5
Caster Clo. SG1	11 H5
Cavell Walk. SG2	16 C3
Cavendish Rd. SG1	14 D3
Caxton Way. SG1	15 E5
Chadwell La. SG1	15 E5
Chalkdown. SG2	17 E2
Chambers Gate. SG1	15 G2
Chancellors Rd. SG1	12 B5
Chapman Rd. SG1	12 A6
Chatsworth Ct. SG2	18 C2
Chauncy Rd. SG1	15 H3
Chells La. SG2	16 D2
Chells Way. SG2	16 B2
Chepstow Clo. SG1	16 C1
Chequers Bridge Rd. SG1	15 F3

Cherry Clo. SG3	20 B3
Cherry Trees Dri. SG2	16 B2
Chertsey Rise. SG2	16 C5
Cherwell Dri. SG1	13 F4
Chester Rd. SG1	13 F5
Chestnut Walk. SG1	12 C6
Cholwell Rd. SG2	16 C6
Chouler Gdns. SG1	12 B5
Christie Rd. SG2	16 D4
Church La, Graveley. SG4	12 B2
Church La, Stevenage. SG1	15 F2
Claymores. SG1	15 H3
Cleveland Way. SG1	13 G3
Clevis Croft. SG1	15 H4
Clovelly Way. SG1	14 D2
Colestrete. SG1	16 A5
Colestrete Clo. SG1	16 A4
Collenswood Rd. SG2	16 C5
Colts Cnr. SG2	16 B5
Columbus Clo. SG2	16 B2
Colwyn Clo. SG1	15 E2
Conifer Walk. SG2	16 D2
Constantine Clo. SG1	12 D6
Cook Rd. SG2	16 C2
Coopers Clo. SG2	17 E4
Coreys Mill La. SG1	12 A5
Cornfields. SG2	16 D2
Corton Clo. SG1	12 A6
Cotney Croft. SG1	16 D6
Coventry Clo. SG1	13 F5
Crabtree Rd. SG3	20 B3
Cragside. SG2	19 F5
Crompton Rd. SG1	14 D3
Cromwell Rd. SG1	16 D4
Crossgates. SG1	15 H4
Cuttys La. SG1	15 G4

Street	Ref
Daltry Clo. SG1	12 B5
Daltry Rd. SG1	12 B5
Dancote. SG3	20 B2
Danesgate. SG1	15 G4
Danestrete. SG1	15 G4
Darwin Rd. SG2	16 C3
Dawlish Clo. SG2	19 F4
Deanscroft. SG3	20 B2
Deard's End La. SG3	20 B2
Deards Wood. SG3	20 B2
Deeping Clo. SG3	20 B3
Dene La. SG2	19 G1
Denton Rd. SG1	15 H5
Derby Way. SG1	13 F6
Devonshire Clo. SG2	18 D3
Dewpond Clo. SG1	15 F1
Ditchmore La. SG1	15 F3
Doncaster Clo. SG1	16 C1
Douglas Dri. SG1	16 B1
Dove Rd. SG1	13 E3
Dovedale. SG2	16 C5
Downlands. SG2	16 D2
Drakes Dri. SG2	16 B2
Drapers Way. SG1	15 F2
Dryden Cres. SG2	16 C1
Dunns Clo. SG1	15 H6
Durham Rd. SG1	13 E5
Dyers La. SG1	14 B5
East Clo. SG1	16 A3
East Gate. SG1	15 G4
East Reach. SG2	18 D1
Eastbourne Av. SG1	14 D3
Eastman Way. SG1	13 G4
Edgeworth Clo. SG2	19 F2
Edison Rd. SG2	16 C3
Edmonds Dri. SG2	17 E5
Elbow La. SG2	19 E3
Elder Way. SG1	15 G6
Eliot Rd. SG2	16 C3
Ellis Av. SG1	15 G1
Elm Walk. SG2	16 C5
Ely Clo. SG1	13 G5
Emperors Gate. SG2	16 D1
Enjakes Clo. SG2	19 E4
Essex Rd. SG1	15 E1
Exchange Rd. SG1	16 A4
Exeter Clo. SG1	13 F5
Fair View. SG1	15 E2
Fairfield Way. SG1	13 G4
Fairlands Way. SG1	15 F4
Fairview Rd. SG1	15 E2
Falcon Clo. SG2	19 G1
Fallowfield. SG2	16 D6
Faraday Rd. SG2	16 B3
Farm Clo. SG1	15 G5
Fawcett Rd. SG2	16 C1
Featherston Rd. SG2	16 D6
Fellowes Way. SG2	18 D2
Ferrier Rd. SG2	16 D3
Fieldfare. SG2	17 E6
Filey Clo. SG1	14 D2
Finches End. SG2	17 H1
Fir Clo. SG2	18 D2
Fishers Grn. SG1	14 D1
Fishers Grn La. SG1	12 A6
Fishers Grn Rd. SG1	15 E1
Fleetwood Cres. SG1	15 E2
Flinders Clo. SG2	16 D4
Forest Row. SG2	18 C2
Fortuna Clo. SG1	16 D1
Foster Clo. SG1	12 B5
Four Acres. SG1	15 G2
Fox Rd. SG1	15 H5
Foxfield. SG2	16 D6
Foyle Clo. SG1	13 G4
Franklins Rd. SG1	15 F1
Fred Millard Ct. SG1	15 H4
Frobisher Dri. SG2	16 C2
Fry Rd. SG2	16 C4
Fulton Clo. SG1	15 F4
Furzedown. SG2	16 C5
Garden Field. SG2	19 H1
Garden Walk. SG1	15 H4
Gates Way. SG1	15 F3
George Leighton Ct. SG2	16 B4
Gibbons Way. SG3	20 B2
Gipsy La. SG3	20 A2
Glenwood Clo. SG2	19 F2
Gloucester Clo. SG1	12 D5
Goddard End. SG2	19 F3
Godfrey Clo. SG2	16 C6
Gonville Cres. SG2	19 F1
Gordian Way. SG1	13 H6
Gordons Ct. SG3	20 C2
Gorleston Clo. SG1	11 H6
Grace Way. SG1	15 H1
Granby Rd. SG1	12 B5
Grasmere. SG1	13 H4
Grass Meadows. SG2	16 D2
Graveley La. SG4	12 A1
Graveley Rd. SG4	12 A4
Great Ashby Way. SG1	12 D5
Green Acres. SG2	19 F2
Green Clo. SG2	18 D2
Green St. SG1	15 F2
Greenfield Rd. SG1	15 G2
Greenway. SG2	17 H1
Greenways. SG1	15 G3
Grenville Way. SG2	18 D2
Gresley Way. SG2	16 D4
Greydells Rd. SG1	15 G2
Grinders End. SG4	12 A3
Grove Rd. SG1	15 F2
Guildford Clo. SG1	12 D5
Gun La. SG3	20 B2
Gun Meadow Av. SG3	20 C3
Gun Rd. SG3	20 B3
Gun Rd Gdns. SG3	20 B3
Gunnel's Wood Rd. SG1	15 E2
Haddon Clo. SG2	19 F4
Hadrians Walk. SG1	16 D1
Hadwell Clo. SG1	16 B6
Hammond Clo. SG1	15 G3
Hampton Clo. SG2	19 F4
Hanover Clo. SG1	18 C2
Hardwick Clo. SG2	19 F4
Harefield. SG2	19 F1
Harrow Ct. SG1	15 G4
Harrowdene. SG1	16 C5
Harvest La. SG2	16 D2
Harvey Rd. SG2	16 C3
Hastings Clo. SG1	14 D1
Haycroft Rd. SG1	15 G2
Hayfield. SG2	16 D2
Haygarth. SG3	20 C3
Hayley Common. SG2	16 C5
Hazlemere Rd. SG2	18 D3
Headingley Clo. SG1	15 H1
Hedgerow Clo. SG2	16 D1
Hellards Rd. SG1	15 G2
Herne Rd. SG1	12 A5
Hertford Rd. SG2	18 C3
Higgins Wk. SG1	12 B6
High Plash. SG1	15 G4
High St, Graveley. SG4	12 B2
High St, Stevenage Old Town. SG1	15 F1
Highfield Ct. SG1	15 H2
Hill Mead. SG1	16 A3
Hill Side. SG1	16 A4
Hillcrest. SG1	16 A4
Hilton Clo. SG1	15 E2
Hitchin Rd, Corey's Mill. SG1	12 A4
Hitchin Rd, Stevenage Old Town. SG1	15 F1
Holders La. SG2	17 F4
Holly Copse. SG1	16 A4
Holly Leys. SG2	19 E3
Holly Shaws. SG2	19 E2
Homestead Moat. SG1	15 H4
Hopton Rd. SG1	14 D1
Hornbeam Spring. SG3	20 B3
Hudson Rd. SG1	16 C1
Humber Ct. SG1	13 E3
Hunters Clo. SG2	16 D2
Huntingdon Rd. SG1	15 E1
Hyde Grn. SG1	16 C6
Hydean Way. SG2	16 B6

INDUSTRIAL & RETAIL:

Street	Ref
Argyle Way Ind Est. SG1	15 F4
Bowman Trading Est. SG1	15 E4
Enterprise Park. SG1	15 E2
Gunnels Wood Rd Ind Est. SG1	15 F6
Hyatt Ind Est. SG1	14 D4
Kings Park Ind Est. SG1	15 F5
Marymead Ind Est. SG2	19 E3
Meadway Technology Park. SG1	15 G6
Monkswood Retail Park. SG1	15 G6
Pin Green Ind Area. SG1	13 G5
Roaring Meg Retail Park. SG1	15 G6
Westgate Shopping Centre. SG1	15 G4

Street	Ref
Ingelheim Ct. SG1	15 G2
Ingleside Dri. SG1	12 A5
Inns Clo. SG1	15 F3
Inskip Cres. SG1	15 H3
Iona Clo. SG1	13 E5
Islington Way. SG1	12 D5
Ivel Rd. SG1	15 F2
Jackdaw Clo. SG2	16 D4
James Way. SG1	15 F2
Jennings Clo. SG2	15 G6
Jessop Rd. SG1	13 E6
Jubilee Rd. SG1	15 E1
Julia Gate. SG2	16 D1
Julians Clo. SG1	15 F1
Julians Rd. SG1	15 E1
Jupiter Gate. SG2	16 D1
Keats Clo. SG2	16 C2
Keith Wood. SG3	20 B2
Keller Clo. SG2	16 C4
Kenilworth Clo. SG2	19 F4
Kenmare Clo. SG2	19 F4
Kennett Way. SG1	13 E4
Kerr Clo. SG3	20 B2
Kessingland Av. SG1	11 H6
Kestrel Clo. SG2	19 G1
Kimbolton Cres. SG2	18 C3
King George Clo. SG1	15 G3
Kingfisher Rise. SG2	19 G1
Kings Rd. SG1	15 H2
Kings Walden Rise. SG2	16 D1
Kings Way. SG1	15 F5
Kitching La. SG2	14 D4
Knights Templars Grn. SG2	16 D1
Kymswell Rd. SG2	16 C5
Lancaster Clo. SG1	12 D5
Langthorne Av. SG1	15 H2
Lanterns La. SG2	17 E3
Lapwing Rise. SG2	17 E6
Larkinson. SG1	15 E2
Larwood Gro. SG1	16 A1
Lawrence Av. SG1	15 H2
Leaves Spring. SG2	18 D1
Legget Gro. SG1	15 H1
Leslie Clo. SG2	19 F1
Letchmore Clo. SG1	15 G2
Letchmore Rd. SG1	15 F3
Leyden Rd. SG1	18 A1
Lime Clo. SG2	17 E5
Lincoln Rd. SG1	13 F4
Lingfield Rd. SG1	13 G6
Linkways. SG1	16 A4
Lintott Clo. SG1	15 F3
Lismore. SG2	19 F2
Little Hyde. SG2	16 C5
Livingstone Link. SG2	16 C1
Lodge Way. SG2	18 D2
Lomond Way. SG1	13 H4
London Rd, Knebworth. SG3	20 C3
London Rd, Stevenage. SG1	15 G5
Long Hyde. SG2	16 C5
Long La. SG2	17 E4
Long Leaves. SG2	18 D1
Long Ridge. SG2	19 G2
Longcroft Rd. SG2	15 G2
Longfields. SG2	19 F2
Lonsdale Ct. SG1	16 A2
Lonsdale Rd. SG1	16 A1
Lower Sean. SG2	16 B6
Lowes Clo. SG1	13 H4
Lygrave. SG2	19 F3
Lymington Rd. SG1	15 E1
Lyndale. SG1	15 H5
Lytton Fields. SG3	20 B2
Lytton Way. SG1	15 F1
MacKenzie Sq. SG2	16 C6
Made Feld. SG1	15 H4
Magellan Clo. SG2	16 D4
Magpie Cres. SG2	16 D5
Mallard Rd. SG2	19 G1
Malvern Clo. SG2	19 E4
Manchester Clo. SG1	13 E4
Mandeville. SG2	19 A3
Manor View. SG2	19 E2
Marcus Clo. SG1	16 D1
Market Pl. SG1	15 G4
Market Sq. SG1	15 G4
Marlborough Rd. SG2	16 C1
Marlowe Rd. SG2	16 C1
Marshgate. SG1	15 G4
Martins Way. SG1	12 B6
Marymead Ct. SG2	18 D3
Marymead Dri. SG2	18 D3
Mathews Clo. SG1	12 C5
Maxwell Rd. SG1	15 E4
Mayles Clo. SG1	15 E1
Maypole Ct. SG2	19 F4
Mead Clo. SG1	16 A3
Meadow Way. SG1	16 A4
Meadway, Knebworth. SG3	20 B3
Meadway, Stevenage. SG1	15 E3
Medalls Link. SG2	16 B6
Medalls Path. SG2	16 B6
Melne Rd. SG2	19 E3
Meredith Rd. SG1	16 A1
Middle Row. SG1	15 F2
Middlesboro Clo. SG1	13 E4
Mildmay Rd. SG1	13 F6
Milestone Clo. SG2	17 E5
Milestone Rd. SG3	20 C2
Minehead Way. SG1	14 D2
Minerva Clo. SG1	13 H6
Minsden Rd. SG1	17 E6
Mobbsbury Way. SG2	16 C1
Monks View. SG2	28 C1
Monks Wood Rd. SG1	15 G5
Morecambe Clo. SG1	15 E2
Morgan Clo. SG1	12 C5
Mount Keen. SG1	13 H3
Mountfitchet Wk. SG2	16 D1
Mozart Ct. SG1	15 E4
Muirhead Way. SG2	20 B2
Mundesley Clo. SG1	12 A6
Nash Clo. SG2	16 B3
Neagh Clo. SG1	13 H4
Neptune Gate. SG1	13 H6
New Clo. SG3	20 B1
Newbury Clo. SG1	12 C5
Newcastle Clo. SG1	13 E4
Newgate. SG2	16 B5
Newlyn Clo. SG1	14 D3
Newpark La. SG2	19 H1
Newton Rd. SG2	16 B3
Nicholas Pl. SG1	12 C6
Nightingale Walk. SG2	16 C4
Nodes Dri. SG2	18 D3
Nokeside. SG2	19 E3
North Rd. SG1	12 B4
Norton Grn Rd. SG1	15 F5
Norton Rd. SG1	15 F5
Norwich Clo. SG1	13 F5
Nursery Clo. SG1	18 D3
Oak La. SG4	12 A2
Oakfield Clo. SG2	19 F2
Oakfields. SG2	19 F2
Oakfields Av. SG3	20 C1
Oakfields Rd. SG3	20 C1
Oaks Cross. SG2	19 E2
Oakwell Clo. SG2	19 G4
Oakwood Clo. SG2	19 F1
Old Bourne Way. SG1	13 E4
Old Knebworth La. SG1	18 A5
Old La. SG3	20 C2
Olde Swann Ct. SG1	15 F1
Orchard Cres. SG1	15 F2
Orchard Rd. SG1	15 E1
Orchard Way. SG3	20 B2
Orwell Av. SG1	13 E4
Osprey Gdns. SG2	19 G1
Osterley Clo. SG2	19 F4
Oundle Path. SG2	19 F3
Oxleys Rd. SG2	16 C6
Pacatian Way. SG1	16 D1
Paddocks Clo. SG2	16 B5
Pankhurst Cres. SG2	16 C4
Parishes Mead. SG2	17 E5
Park Clo. SG2	19 E2
Park La. SG3	20 A2
Park Pl. SG1	15 G4
Park View. SG2	19 E2
Parkers Field. SG2	16 C5
Parkway. SG2	18 D2
Parsons Grn. SG1	13 G4
Peartree Way. SG2	16 B6
Penn Rd. SG1	15 G5
Pentland Rise. SG1	13 G4
Pepsal End. SG2	19 E3
Peter Way. SG3	20 B1
Petworth Clo. SG2	19 F4
Pike End. SG1	15 G2
Pilgrims Way. SG1	13 F5
Pinewoods. SG2	18 C2
Plash Dri. SG1	15 H4
Pollard Gdns. SG1	16 A1
Pond Clo. SG1	15 F2
Pond Side. SG4	12 B3
Pondcroft Rd. SG3	20 C2
Popple Way. SG1	15 G3
Poppymead. SG1	16 A5
Potters La. SG1	15 E5
Pound Av. SG1	15 G3
Prestatyn Clo. SG1	15 E1
Primett Rd. SG1	15 F2
Primrose Ct. SG1	15 G2
Primrose Hill Rd. SG1	15 G2
Priory Dell. SG1	15 H4
Providence Gro. SG1	15 H1
Quantock Clo. SG1	13 H4
Queensway. SG1	15 G4
Raban Clo. SG2	19 F2
Raleigh Cres. SG2	16 B2
Ramsdell. SG1	16 A4
Randals Hill. SG2	16 C6
Ranworth Av. SG2	19 F4
Rectory Croft. SG1	12 C5
Rectory La. SG1	12 B6
Redcar Dri. SG1	14 D3
Redwing Clo. SG2	16 D5
Riccart La. SG1	13 E3
Ridgeway. SG1	16 A3
Ridlins End. SG2	19 F1
Ripon Rd. SG1	13 E5
Rockingham Way. SG1	15 H6
Roebuck Gate. SG2	18 C2
Rooks Nest Farm Barns. SG1	12 D5
Rookwood Dri. SG2	19 E2
Roundmead. SG2	16 D6
Rowan Cres. SG1	15 G2
Rowland Rd. SG1	15 H5
Rowland Rd Nth. SG1	15 H5
Rowland Rd Sth. SG1	15 H5
Ruckles Clo. SG1	15 H4
Rudd Clo. SG2	19 E1
Russell Clo. SG2	19 E2
Rutherford Clo. SG1	14 D3
Ryders Hill. SG2	13 H4
Rye Clo. SG1	13 E4
Ryecroft. SG1	15 H2
St Albans Dri. SG1	12 D5
St Albans Link. SG1	12 D5
St Andrews Dri. SG1	12 D4
St Davids Clo. SG1	13 E4
St George's Way. SG1	15 G4
St Margarets. SG2	18 C1
St Martins La. SG3	20 C2
St Marys Clo. SG1	19 H1
Salisbury Rd. SG1	13 F4
Sandown Rd. SG1	13 G6
Sayer Way. SG3	20 B3
Scarborough Av. SG1	14 D1
School Clo. SG2	16 C6
School La. SG2	19 H1
Scott Rd. SG2	16 C3
Sefton Rd. SG1	13 F6
Senate Pl. SG1	13 G4
Serpentine Clo. SG1	13 H4
Severn Way. SG1	13 E4
Shackle Dell. SG2	18 D1
Shackleton Spring. SG2	16 A6
Shaftesbury Ct. SG1	15 G5
Sheafgreen La. SG2	17 E4
Shearwater Clo. SG2	16 D5
Sheepcroft Hill. SG2	16 D6
Shephall Grn. SG2	19 E1
Shephall Grn La. SG2	19 E2
Shephall La. SG2	18 D2
Shephall View. SG1	16 A5
Shephall Way. SG2	16 C5
Shepherds La. SG1	14 C3
Sheringham Rd. SG1	12 A6
Shirley Clo. SG1	16 C1
Shoreham Clo. SG1	14 D1
Short La. SG2	17 F5
Siddons Rd. SG2	16 D3
Silam Rd. SG1	15 G4
Sinfield Clo. SG1	16 B4
Sish Clo. SG1	15 G3

Street	Ref.
Sish La. SG1	15 F3
Sisson Clo. SG2	19 F1
Six Hills Way. SG2	15 F5
Skegness Rd. SG1	14 D1
Skipton Clo. SG2	18 C3
Skylark Cnr. SG2	17 E6
Sleaps Hyde. SG2	19 F2
South Gate. SG1	15 G5
Southend Clo. SG1	15 F2
Southsea Rd. SG1	15 E1
Southwold Clo. SG1	14 D3
Southwark Clo. SG1	13 F5
Sparrow Dri. SG2	16 D5
Speke Clo. SG2	16 D4
Spring Dri. SG2	18 D3
Stafford Ct. SG3	20 C2
Stanley Rd. SG2	16 B1
Stanmore Rd. SG1	15 F2
Station Rd. SG3	20 B2
Stevenage Rd, Knebworth. SG3	20 B1
Stevenage Rd, Walkern. SG2	17 E1
Stirling Clo. SG2	19 F4
Stobarts Clo. SG3	20 B1
Stockens Dell. SG3	20 B3
Stockens Grn. SG3	20 B3
Stonecroft. SG3	20 B2
Stony Croft. SG1	15 H3
Stringers La. SG2	19 H2
Sutcliffe Clo. SG1	16 A1
Swale Clo. SG1	13 E3
Swangleys La. SG3	20 C2
Sweynes Mead. SG2	16 D1
Swingate. SG1	15 F4
Symonds Grn La. SG1	14 D2
Symonds Grn Rd. SG1	14 D1
Tacitus Clo. SG1	16 D1
Tamar Clo. SG1	13 E4
Tates Way. SG1	12 A5
Tatlers La. SG2	17 E4
Taywood Clo. SG2	19 E1
Tees Clo. SG1	13 E3
Telford Av. SG2	16 B3
The Avenue. SG1	15 F1
The Brambles. SG1	12 C5
The Chace. SG2	18 C2
The Chilterns. SG1	13 G3
The Close. SG1	12 B6
The Dell. SG1	15 H3
The Forum. SG1	15 G4
The Glynde. SG2	19 E3
The Grange. SG2	15 F1
The Hawthorns. SG1	16 A5
The Hedgerows. SG2	16 D1
The Hornbeams. SG2	16 C5
The Hyde. SG2	16 C6
The Lawns. SG2	16 D5
The Lindens. SG1	15 H5
The Maltings. SG2	17 H1
The Muntings. SG2	16 B6
The Noke. SG2	19 E3
The Old Walled Garden. SG1	12 B5
The Oundle. SG2	19 F3
The Paddocks. SG2	16 C5
The Pastures. SG2	16 D1
The Quadrant. SG1	15 G4
The Ridings. SG2	16 B5
The Spinney. SG2	16 D2
The Spur. SG1	15 H5
The White Way. SG2	16 D2
The Willows. SG2	18 D3
Thirlmere. SG1	13 H5
Thornbury Clo. SG2	18 D3
Thurlow Clo. SG1	12 C5
Tillers Link. SG2	18 D1
Tintern Clo. SG2	19 E4
Tippet Clo. SG1	15 G6
Titmus Clo. SG1	15 H3
Torquay Cres. SG1	15 E2
Towers Rd. SG1	15 G5
Town Sq. SG1	15 G4
Trafford Clo. SG1	12 D6
Trajan Gate. SG1	13 H6
Trent Clo. SG1	12 D6
Trigg Ter. SG1	15 H3
Trinity Pl. SG1	15 F3
Trinity Rd. SG1	15 F3
Trumper Rd. SG1	12 D6
Tudor Clo. SG1	12 B6
Turner Clo. SG1	12 B5
Turpins Rise. SG2	18 C2
Twin Woods. SG1	16 A5
Tye End. SG2	19 E3
Ullswater. SG1	13 H5
Underwood Rd. SG1	12 B5
Unwin Pl. SG1	16 C6
Uplands. SG2	17 E1
Upper Sean. SG2	16 B6
Valerian Way. SG1	13 H6
Vallans Gate. SG2	19 E2
Valley Way. SG2	18 C1
Vardon Rd. SG1	16 B1
Verity Way. SG1	13 F6
Victoria Clo. SG1	15 F2
Vinters Av. SG1	16 A4
Wadnall Way. SG3	20 B3
Walden End. SG1	15 H5
Walkern Rd. SG1	15 F2
Walkern Rd. SG2	17 G6
Walnut Tree Clo. SG2	17 E4
Walsham Clo. SG2	19 F4
Wansbeck Clo. SG1	13 F4
Warners Clo. SG2	16 C6
Warwick Rd. SG2	16 C3
Watercress Clo. SG2	17 E4
Watton Rd. SG3	20 C2
Waverley Clo. SG2	18 D3
Webb Rise. SG1	16 A2
Wedgewood Ct. SG1	13 G4
Wedgewood Gate. SG1	13 G5
Wedgewood Way. SG1	13 G5
Wellington Rd. SG2	16 D4
Wensum Rd. SG1	13 E3
West Clo. SG1	16 A3
West Reach. SG2	18 D1
Westland Rd. SG3	20 B2
Weston Rd, Pin Green. SG1	12 D6
Weston Rd, St Nicholas. SG1	13 F3
Wetherby Clo. SG1	13 G6
Wheatlands. SG2	16 D2
White La. SG1	14 A3
Whitesmead Rd. SG1	15 G2
Whitney Dri. SG1	12 B5
Whittington La. SG1	15 H5
Whitworth Rd. SG1	13 G4
Whomerley Rd. SG1	15 H5
Wigram Way. SG2	16 C5
Wildwood La. SG1	15 H6
William Pl. SG2	16 B6
Willows Link. SG2	18 D3
Wilson Clo. SG1	12 C5
*Wilton Cotts, Church La. SG1	15 F2
Wiltshire Rd. SG2	16 B5
Winchester Clo. SG1	13 F4
Windermere. SG1	13 H5
Windrush Clo. SG1	13 F3
Windsor Clo. SG2	19 E4
Wisden Rd. SG1	13 E6
Woburn Clo. SG2	19 F4
Wood Dri. SG2	19 E2
Woodcock Rd. SG2	19 G1
Woodfield Rd. SG1	12 B5
Woodland Way. SG2	18 C2
Woolners Way. SG1	15 F3
Wortham Way. SG2	19 E1
Wren Clo. SG2	16 C3
Wrights Mdw. SG2	17 H1
Wrights Orchard. SG2	19 H1
Wychdell. SG2	19 F3
Yarmouth Rd. SG1	14 D2
Yeomans Dri. SG2	19 H2
York Rd. SG1	12 D5

HITCHIN

Street	Ref.
Abbis Orchard. SG5	3 D2
Acre Piece. SG5	8 D5
Alexandra Rd. SG5	8 D2
Alpine Clo. SG4	9 E6
Arch Rd. SG4	11 E3
Arlesey Rd. SG5	3 C3
Armour Rise. SG4	9 F1
Arnold Clo. SG4	9 E3
Ash Dri. SG4	10 B3
Ashbrook La. SG4	10 C4
Aston Rise. SG4	9 F5
Baliol Rd. SG5	8 D2
Balmoral Rd. SG5	8 C2
Bancroft. SG5	8 C4
Bearton Av. SG5	8 C3
Bearton Grn. SG5	8 B2
Bearton Rd. SG5	8 B2
Beaumont Clo. SG5	8 B2
Bedford Rd, Ickleford. SG5	3 B1
Bedford Rd, Westmill. SG5	8 B1
Bedford St. SG5	8 B3
Beechwood Clo. SG5	8 B1
Bell Clo. SG4	9 F5
Benchley Hill. SG4	9 G3
Benslow La. SG4	8 D3
Benslow Rise. SG4	9 E3
Berkeley Clo. SG5	8 B3
Bessemer Clo. SG5	3 C4
Biggin La. SG5	8 C4
Bilton Rd. SG4	8 D1
Bingen Rd. SG5	8 A2
Blackhorse Clo. SG4	10 B2
Blackhorse La. SG4	10 B2
Bladon Clo. SG4	11 G3
Blakemore End Rd. SG4	11 E5
Boswell Dri. SG5	3 C3
Bowmans Av. SG4	9 F4
Bowyers Clo. SG5	8 B2
Bradleys Cnr. SG4	9 G2
Bramfield. SG4	9 F4
Brampton Park Rd. SG5	8 C2
Bramshott Clo. SG4	10 A2
Brand St. SG5	8 C4
Brick Kiln La. SG4	10 A2
Bridge St. SG5	8 C5
Broad Meadow Rise. SG4	10 B3
Broadmead. SG4	9 E5
Brookview. SG4	9 F5
Browning Dri. SG4	9 F3
Bucklersbury. SG5	8 C4
Bunyan Rd. SG5	8 C3
Burford Way. SG5	8 A1
Burns Clo. SG4	9 E3
Bury Mead Rd. SG5	8 D1
Byron Clo. SG4	9 E3
Cadwell La. SG5	8 D1
Cam Sq. SG4	3 E4
Cambridge Rd. SG4	9 F2
Campbell Clo. SG4	9 F3
Castle Ct. SG4	8 B2
Cedar Av. SG5	3 C3
Cemetery Rd. SG4	8 D5
Chalkdell Path. SG5	8 B3
Chambers La. SG5	3 C3
Chantry La. SG4	11 G4
Charlton Rd. SG5	8 B6
Chaucer Way. SG4	9 F3
Chennells Clo. SG4	9 F1
Chestnut Clo. SG5	8 B3
Chestnut Walk. SG4	10 B2
Chiltern Rd. SG4	9 E4
Church Path, Ickleford. SG5	3 C3
Church Path, Little Wymondley. SG4	11 G3
Church Rd. SG5	8 C4
Churchyard Walk. SG5	8 C4
Claymore Dri. SG5	3 D2
Coach Dri. SG4	10 A2
Coleridge Clo. SG4	9 F3
College Rd. SG5	8 D3
Collison Clo. SG4	9 F1
Common Rise. SG4	9 E2
Conquest Clo. SG4	10 B2
Convent Clo. SG5	8 D3
Cooks Way. SG4	9 E2
Cranborne Av. SG5	8 B5
Crow Furlong. SG5	8 B4
Cubitt Clo. SG4	9 F4
Dacre Rd. SG5	9 E3
Dale Clo. SG4	10 A2
Deacons Way. SG5	8 B2
Desborough Rd. SG4	9 F2
Dower Ct. SG4	10 A2
Dugdale Ct. SG5	8 A2
Dukes La. SG5	8 C3
Duncots Clo. SG5	3 C3
East Clo. SG4	9 F2
East View. SG4	10 D4
Elderberry Dri. SG4	10 B2
Elms Clo. SG4	11 F3
Elmside Walk. SG5	8 C3
Eynsford Ct. SG4	8 D5
Fairfield Way. SG4	9 G3
Fells Clo. SG5	8 D3
Firs Clo. SG5	8 B3
Fishponds Rd. SG5	8 C3
Florence St. SG5	8 D3
Folly Clo. SG4	8 D6
Folly Path. SG4	8 D5
Forge Clo. SG5	8 D3
Fosman Clo. SG5	8 B3
Foster Dri. SG4	10 B2
Francis Clo. SG4	10 B2
Franklin Gdns. SG4	9 F2
Freemans Clo. SG5	8 B2
Freewaters Clo. SG5	3 C3
French Lodge. SG5	8 D3
Frensham Dri. SG4	9 G1
Friday Furlong. SG5	8 B3
Gainsford Cres. SG4	9 F1
Galley Wood. SG5	3 C3
Gaping La. SG5	8 B4
Garden Row. SG5	8 D3
Gibson Clo. SG4	9 F3
Girdle Rd. SG4	9 E1
Girons Clo. SG4	9 E4
Gosmore Ley Clo. SG4	10 A3
Gosmore Rd. SG4	10 A2
Grammar School Wk. SG5	8 C4
Grange Clo. SG4	10 B2
Granville Rd. SG4	9 G2
Graveley La. SG4	11 G1
Graveley Rd. SG4	11 F1
Grays La. SG5	8 B4
Green La. SG4	9 F2
Greenfield Av. SG5	3 C3
Greenfield La. SG5	3 C3
Greenside Dri. SG5	8 B3
Grimstone Rd. SG4	11 F3
Grove Rd. SG5	8 D2
Grovelands Av. SG4	9 F1
Half Acre. SG5	8 B5
Halsey Dri. SG4	9 F4
Hambridge Way. SG5	3 A3
Hampden Rd. SG4	9 F2
Hardy Clo. SG4	9 F4
Harkness Ct. SG4	9 F2
Harkness Way. SG4	9 F1
Harrison Clo. SG4	8 D4
Hartland Ct. SG5	8 B4
Hawthorne Clo. SG5	8 B5
Hazelwood Clo. SG5	8 D3
Heathfield Rd. SG5	8 C1
Hensley Clo. SG4	9 F4
Hermitage Rd. SG5	8 C4
High Dane. SG4	9 E1
High St, Gosmore. SG4	10 A4
High St, Hitchin. SG5	8 C4
High View. SG5	8 B4
Highbury Rd. SG4	8 D4
Highover Way. SG4	9 E2
Hill Path. SG4	10 A2
Hillfield Av. SG4	9 E1
Hillgate. SG5	3 E3
Hine Way. SG5	8 A2
Hitchin Hill. SG4	8 D5
Hitchin Rd, Gosmore. SG4	10 A3
Hitchin Rd, Oakfield. SG4	9 G5
Holdbrook. SG4	9 F4
Holden Clo. SG4	9 F4
Hollow La. SG4	8 D4
Hunting Gate. SG5	3 E4
Ibberson Way. SG4	9 E4
Ickleford Rd. SG5	8 D2
Icknield Clo. SG5	3 C3
Ivatt Ct. SG4	9 F4
Jill Grey Pl. SG5	8 C4
John Barker Pl. SG5	8 A2
Kardwell Clo. SG4	9 E5
Keats Way. SG4	9 F4
Kendale Rd. SG4	8 D5
Kershaws Hill. SG4	8 D4
Kingfisher Ct. SG4	9 E5
King Georges Clo. SG5	8 B1
Kings Hedges. SG5	8 A2
Kings Rd. SG5	8 D2
Kingsdown. SG4	9 F4
Kingswood Av. SG4	9 G2
Kipling Clo. SG4	9 G4
Knowl Piece. SG5	3 E4
Lammas Mead. SG5	8 C1
Lancaster Av. SG5	8 B2
Lancaster Rd. SG5	8 C2
Langbridge Clo. SG4	10 B2
Larch Av. SG4	10 B3
Latchmore Clo. SG4	8 D5
Laurel Way. SG5	3 C3
Lavender Way. SG5	8 B3
Lindsay Av. SG4	9 E6
Linten Clo. SG4	9 F5
Lister Av. SG4	10 A2
Lodge Ct. SG5	3 C3
London Rd. SG4	10 A2
Long Meadow Dri. SG5	3 D2
Lovell Clo. SG4	9 E5
Lower Innings. SG5	8 B3
Lucas La. SG5	8 B4
Lyles Row. SG4	8 D4
Manor Clo. SG5	3 C3
Manor Cres. SG4	9 E5
Manton Rd. SG4	9 F5
Market Pl. SG5	8 C4
Masefield. SG4	9 G4
Matthew Gate. SG4	10 B2
Mattocke Rd. SG5	8 A2
Maxwells Path. SG5	8 B3
May Trees. SG4	9 E5
Maydencroft La. SG4	10 A4
Maylin Clo. SG4	9 G3
Meadow Bank. SG4	9 E2
Meadow Way. SG5	8 B5
Mermaid Clo. SG4	9 F4
Milestone Rd. SG5	8 B2
Mill Clo. SG4	9 G3
Mill La. SG4	10 A4
Mill Rd. SG4	10 B4
Millard Way. SG4	9 F1
Millfield La. SG4	10 B3
Millstream Clo. SG4	8 D1
Milton Vw. SG4	9 G4
Moormead Clo. SG5	8 B5
Moormead Hill. SG5	8 A5
Moss Way. SG5	8 A2
Mount Garrison. SG4	8 D4
Mount Pleasant. SG5	8 B5
Mountjoy. SG4	9 G2
Mowbray Gdns. SG4	10 B2
Mulberry Way. SG5	8 B1
New England. SG4	10 B3
Newlands Clo E. SG4	10 B2
Newlands Clo W. SG4	10 A3
Newlands La. SG4	10 A3
Newtons Way. SG4	8 D5
Nightingale Rd. SG5	8 D3
Nimbus Way. SG4	9 F4
Nine Springs Way. SG4	9 F5
North Pl. SG5	8 B2
Nuns Clo. SG5	8 C4
Nutleigh Gro. SG5	8 B2
Oakfield Av. SG4	9 E6
Oaks Clo. SG4	10 A2
Offley Rd. SG5	8 A5
Old Bakery. SG5	8 B4
Old Chantry La. SG4	11 G4
Old Charlton Rd. SG5	8 C5
Old Hale Way, Ickleford. SG5	3 C3
Old Hale Way, Westmill. SG5	8 C2
Old Park Rd. SG5	8 C4
Orchard Clo. SG4	10 B4
Orchard Rd. SG4	9 F2
Orlando Clo. SG4	9 E5
Oughton Clo. SG5	8 B3
Oughtonhead La. SG5	8 A3
Oughtonhead Way. SG5	8 B3
Park St. SG4	8 C5
Park Way. SG4	8 C4
Parkgate. SG4	8 C5
Passingham Av. SG4	9 E5
Paynes Pk. SG5	8 C4
Peppercorn Wk. SG4	9 F4
Periwinkle La. SG5	8 D2
Pirton Clo. SG5	8 B4
Pirton Rd. SG5	8 A4
Poplar Clo. SG4	9 E5
Portman Clo. SG5	8 B1
Portmill La. SG5	8 C4
Preston Rd. SG4	10 A6
Priory Ct. SG4	8 D6
Priory End. SG4	8 C5
Priory La. SG4	11 F3

Priory View. SG4 — 11 F3
Priory Way. SG4 — 10 A2
Pullman Dri. SG4 — 9 F4
Pulters Way. SG4 — 8 D5
Purwell La. SG4 — 9 F3

Queen St. SG4 — 8 D5
Queenswood Dri. SG4 — 9 G2

Radcliffe Rd. SG5 — 8 D3
Ransom Clo. SG4 — 10 A2
Redhill Rd. SG5 — 8 A3
Redoubt Clo. SG4 — 9 E2
Regal Ct. SG5 — 8 D3
Riddy Hill Clo. SG4 — 9 E5
Riddy La. SG4 — 9 E5
River Ct. SG5 — 3 D2
River Mead. SG5 — 8 A1
Roundwood Clo. SG4 — 9 G1
Rowan Gro. SG4 — 10 B2
Ruskin La. SG4 — 9 G4
Russells Slip. SG5 — 8 B5
Ryder Av. SG5 — 3 B4
Ryder Way. SG5 — 3 B4

St Andrews Pl. SG4 — 8 D4
St Annes Rd. SG5 — 8 D3
St Augustine Clo. SG5 — 8 D2
St Elmo Ct. SG4 — 10 A2
St Faiths Clo. SG4 — 9 F2
St Johns Path. SG4 — 8 D5
St Johns Rd. SG4 — 8 D5
St Katharines Clo. SG5 — 3 B3
St Marks Clo. SG5 — 8 C2
St Marys Sq. SG5 — 8 D4
St Michaels Mt. SG4 — 9 E3
St Michaels Rd. SG4 — 9 E3
Sandover Clo. SG4 — 9 F5
Sandy Gro. SG4 — 8 D5
Sanfoine Clo. SG4 — 9 G3
Seebohm Clo. SG5 — 8 A2
Sharps Way. SG4 — 9 E2
Shelley La. SG4 — 9 G4
Shepherds Mead. SG5 — 8 C1
Siccut Rd. SG4 — 11 F3
Silver Ct. SG5 — 8 C3
Snailswell La. SG5 — 3 C1
Sorrel Garth. SG4 — 9 E4
South Hill Clo. SG4 — 9 E5
South Pl. SG5 — 8 B3
Spellbrooke. SG5 — 8 B3
Sperberry Hill. SG4 — 10 C5
Spinney Clo. SG4 — 9 E4
Spurrs Clo. SG4 — 9 F4
Standhill Clo. SG4 — 8 D5
Standhill Rd. SG4 — 8 D5
Station App. SG4 — 9 E3
Stevenage Rd,
  Hitchin. SG4 — 8 D6
Stevenage Rd, Little
  Wymondley. SG4 — 11 E3
Stevenage Rd,
  St Ippollitts. SG4 — 10 C4
Stirling Clo. SG4 — 9 F4
Storehouse La. SG4 — 8 D5
Stormont Rd. SG5 — 8 D2
Stotfold Rd. SG4 — 9 G1
Strathmore Av. SG5 — 8 C1
Stuart Dri. SG4 — 9 F4
Sturgeons Way. SG4 — 9 E1
Sturrock Way. SG4 — 9 G4
Sun St. SG5 — 8 C4
Sunnyside Rd. SG4 — 8 D5
Swinburne Av. SG5 — 8 A2
Sycamore Clo. SG4 — 10 B2
Symonds Rd. SG5 — 8 B3

Talisman St. SG4 — 9 F4
Tall Trees. SG4 — 10 B2
Talbot St. SG5 — 8 B3
Taylors Hill. SG4 — 8 C5
Tennyson Av. SG4 — 9 G4
Thatchers End. SG4 — 9 G3
The Aspens. SG4 — 9 E5
The Avenue. SG4 — 9 E4
The Beeches. SG4 — 9 E5
The Chapmans. SG5 — 8 C4
The Chilterns. SG4 — 9 E4
The Crescent,
  Gosmore. SG4 — 10 B4
The Crescent,
  Westmill. SG5 — 8 B2
The Finches. SG4 — 9 E4
The Limes. SG5 — 8 B5
The Maples. SG4 — 8 D6
The Mead. SG5 — 8 C1

The Paddock. SG4 — 10 B2
The Poplars. SG5 — 3 D1
The Ridgeway. SG5 — 8 B5
The Willows. SG4 — 10 C2
Thistley La. SG4 — 10 A5
Tilehouse St. SG5 — 8 C4
Times Clo. SG5 — 8 B1
Tower Clo. SG4 — 11 F3
Traherne Clo. SG4 — 8 D6
Trevor Rd. SG4 — 9 E3
Tristram Rd. SG4 — 9 E1
Truemans Rd. SG5 — 8 B1
Tudor Ct. SG5 — 8 B5
Turnpike La. SG5 — 3 B4

Uplands Av. SG4 — 9 F5
Upper Tilehouse St. SG5 — 8 C4

Verulam Rd. SG5 — 8 D3
Victoria Rd. SG5 — 8 B3

Wallace Way. SG4 — 8 D1
Walnut Clo. SG5 — 9 E5
Walnut Way. SG5 — 3 C3
Walsh Clo. SG5 — 8 B4
Walsworth Rd. SG4 — 8 D4
Waltham Rd. SG5 — 8 D5
Water La. SG5 — 8 D2
Waterdell La. SG4 — 10 B4
Waterlow Mews. SG4 — 11 F3
Wedgewood Rd. SG4 — 9 F4
Wedmore Rd. SG4 — 8 D5
Wellingham Av. SG5 — 8 B2
West Alley. SG5 — 8 C4
West Clo. SG4 — 9 F1
West Hill. SG5 — 8 B3
Westbury Clo. SG5 — 8 B3
Westfield Clo. SG5 — 8 B4
Westfield La. SG5 — 8 B4
Westmill La. SG5 — 3 A4
Westmill Rd. SG5 — 8 A1
Westwood Av. SG4 — 9 E5
Whinbush Gro. SG5 — 8 D3
Whinbush Rd. SG5 — 8 D3
Whitegale Clo. SG4 — 9 E5
Whitehill Clo. SG4 — 9 E5
Whitehill Rd. SG4 — 8 D5
Whitehurst Av. SG5 — 8 C2
Wilbury Way. SG4 — 9 E1
Willian Rd. SG4 — 9 F2
Willoughby Way. SG4 — 9 E5
Willow La. SG4 — 8 B5
Willow Tree Way. SG5 — 8 C1
Wilshere Cres. SG4 — 9 G2
Wilton Rd. SG5 — 8 C2
Windmill Hill. SG4 — 8 D4
Windmill La. SG5 — 8 A6
Winston Clo. SG5 — 8 B4
Witter Av. SG5 — 3 C2
Woodcroft. SG5 — 8 C5
Woolgrove Rd. SG4 — 9 E1
Woodside Gdns. SG4 — 8 D4
Worsdell Way. SG4 — 9 F4
Wratten Clo. SG5 — 8 C5
Wratten Rd E. SG5 — 8 C5
Wratten Rd W. SG5 — 8 B4
Wyatt Clo. SG5 — 3 B3
Wymondley Clo. SG4 — 9 E4
Wymondley Rd. SG4 — 9 E4

York Rd. SG5 — 8 C2

LETCHWORTH & BALDOCK

Abbotts Rd. SG6 — 6 B2
Alban Rd. SG6 — 7 G5
Alder Clo. SG7 — 5 G4
Aldridge Ct. SG7 — 5 G3
Allington La. SG6 — 6 D5
Allison. SG6 — 7 F3
Amor Way. SG6 — 7 F2
Anchor Rd. SG7 — 5 G4
Archers Way. SG6 — 6 B2
Arden Press Way. SG6 — 7 E2
Arena Par. SG6 — 6 D3
Arlesey New Rd. SG6 — 6 A1
Ashbourne Clo. SG6 — 7 F5
Ashdown. SG6 — 4 A2
Ashtons La. SG6 — 7 G5
Ashville Way. SG7 — 5 H2
Aubreys. SG6 — 6 D6
Avenue One. SG6 — 7 F1
Avocet. SG6 — 4 A2

Back La. SG7 — 5 F4
Baldock La. SG6 — 7 E6
Baldock Rd. SG6 — 6 D5
Barley Rise. SG7 — 5 H3
Barrington Rd. SG6 — 6 D4
Bayworth. SG6 — 7 F3
Bedford Rd. SG6 — 6 B1
Beech Hill. SG6 — 6 B1
Beechwood Clo. SG7 — 5 G6
Bell Acre. SG6 — 7 F4
Bell Acre Gdns. SG6 — 7 F4
Bell Row. SG7 — 5 G3
Bennett Ct. SG6 — 7 E6
Berkeley. SG6 — 7 E4
Bidwell Clo. SG6 — 7 E3
Birds Hill. SG6 — 7 E2
Bittern Way. SG6 — 4 A2
Blackhorse Rd. SG6 — 4 D3
Blackmore. SG6 — 7 F5
Boscombe Clo. SG6 — 7 F3
Bowershott. SG6 — 7 E4
Bramley Clo. SG7 — 5 G2
Brandles Rd. SG6 — 7 E5
Brewery La. SG7 — 5 F3
Briar Patch La. SG6 — 6 C5
Bridge Rd. SG6 — 4 A5
Broadcroft. SG6 — 6 D6
Broadwater Av. SG6 — 6 C3
Broadwater Dale. SG6 — 6 C3
Broadway. SG6 — 6 C5
Brookside. SG6 — 6 D3
Broughton Hill. SG6 — 7 E3
Burley. SG6 — 4 B1
Burnell Rise. SG6 — 6 B3
Burnell Walk. SG6 — 6 C3
Bursland. SG6 — 6 B2
Bush Spring. SG7 — 5 H3
Butlers Yd. SG7 — 5 G2
Butterfield Ct. SG7 — 5 F3
Bygrave Rd. SG7 — 5 G2
Byrd Walk. SG7 — 5 H4

Cade Clo. SG6 — 4 D2
California. SG7 — 5 G2
Cambridge Rd. SG6 — 6 B6
Campers Av. SG6 — 6 C3
Campers Rd. SG6 — 6 C3
Campers Walk. SG6 — 6 C3
Campfield Way. SG6 — 6 B3
Campus Five. SG6 — 7 G1
Cashio La. SG6 — 4 C2
Caslon Way. SG6 — 4 A2
Chagny Clo. SG6 — 6 C2
Chalk Field. SG6 — 7 G5
Chalk Hills. SG7 — 5 G6
Chaomans. SG6 — 6 D6
Chasten Hill. SG6 — 6 B1
Chatterton. SG6 — 7 F4
Chauncy Gdns. SG7 — 5 H3
Childwick Way. SG6 — 4 A3
Chiltern Rd. SG7 — 5 G5
Chiltern View. SG6 — 6 B3
Chilvers Bank. SG7 — 5 F4
Church La. SG6 — 4 D2
Church St. SG7 — 5 F2
Clare Cres. SG7 — 5 G5
Cloisters Lawn. SG6 — 6 D4
Cloisters Rd. SG6 — 6 D4
Clothall Rd. SG7 — 5 G3
Coachmans La. SG7 — 5 F3
Common View. SG6 — 4 C3
Common View Sq. SG6 — 4 C3
Coopers Field. SG6 — 6 B1
Cowslip Hill. SG6 — 6 C1
Crabtree Dell. SG6 — 7 F5
Crabtree La. SG7 — 5 G5
Creamery Ct. SG6 — 7 G5
Croft La. SG6 — 4 C2
Cromwell Grn. SG6 — 4 C3
Cromwell Rd. SG6 — 4 C3
Cross St. SG6 — 4 B4
Crossleys. SG6 — 4 B1
Curlew Clo. SG6 — 4 A2

Dagnalls. SG6 — 6 D6
Daisy Ct. SG6 — 4 C3
Danescroft. SG6 — 4 B2
David Evans Ct. SG6 — 6 B1
Denby. SG6 — 7 F4
Dents Clo. SG6 — 7 F5
Downlands. SG7 — 5 H3
Dunhams La. SG6 — 7 F2
Dunlin. SG6 — 4 A2

Eagle Ct. SG7 — 5 F2
Earlsmead. SG6 — 6 D5

Eastcheap. SG6 — 6 D3
Eastern Way. SG6 — 4 B3
Eastholm. SG6 — 4 B3
Eastholm Grn. SG6 — 4 B3
Eisenberg Clo. SG7 — 5 H2
Eldefield. SG6 — 6 B1
Ellice. SG6 — 7 F4
Elm Park. SG7 — 5 G3
Elmwood Av. SG7 — 5 G4
Ennismore Clo. SG6 — 7 F5

Farm Clo. SG6 — 4 B2
Farriers Clo SG7 — 5 F2
Farthing Dri. SG6 — 7 F6
Field La. SG6 — 6 D4
Fieldfare. SG6 — 4 A2
Fifth Av. SG6 — 7 G2
Firecrest. SG6 — 4 A3
Fleetwood. SG6 — 7 F4
Flint Rd. SG6 — 5 E3
Football Clo. SG7 — 5 G2
Fouracres. SG6 — 7 E6
Fourth Av. SG6 — 7 G1
Fullers Ct. SG6 — 6 C1
Furlay Clo. SG6 — 6 B1
Furmston Ct. SG6 — 4 C4

Garth Rd. SG6 — 6 D5
Gaunts Way. SG6 — 4 B1
Gernon Rd. SG6 — 6 D3
Gernon Walk. SG6 — 6 D3
Gillison Clo. SG6 — 7 F3
Glebe Rd. SG6 — 4 C4
Golden. SG6 — 7 F4
Gorst Clo. SG6 — 6 C3
Grange Rd. SG6 — 4 B3
Great North Rd. SG7 — 5 F1
Great North Rd. SG4 — 5 G6
Green La,
  Letchworth. SG6 — 7 G1
Green La,
  Norton. SG6 — 4 D2
Greenway. SG6 — 7 E6
Grosvenor Rd. SG7 — 5 G2
Grosvenor Rd West. SG7 — 5 G2

Hadleigh. SG6 — 7 F4
Hadrian Way. SG7 — 7 H1
Hall Mead. SG6 — 6 B2
Hammerdell. SG6 — 6 C1
Hampden Clo. SG6 — 4 C3
Haselfoot. SG6 — 6 C2
Hatch La. SG4 — 5 G6
Hawkfield. SG6 — 4 A3
Hawthorn Hill. SG6 — 4 A4
Haymoor. SG6 — 6 C1
Haysman Clo. SG6 — 4 C4
Heathermere. SG6 — 4 A2
Hibberts Ct. SG6 — 6 C1
High Av. SG6 — 6 B3
High St. SG7 — 5 G3
Highfield. SG6 — 6 B4
Highover Rd. SG6 — 6 B3
Hill Path. SG6 — 7 E2
Hill Top. SG7 — 5 F4
Hillbrow. SG6 — 6 B4
Hillcrest. SG7 — 5 G4
Hillshott. SG7 — 7 E3
Hitchin Rd. SG6 — 6 C5
Hitchin St. SG7 — 5 F3
Holmdale. SG6 — 7 E3
Holroyd Cres. SG7 — 5 G4
Hopewell Rd. SG7 — 5 F3
Horace Gay Gdns. SG6 — 6 C3
Howard Dri. SG6 — 7 E5
Howard Gate. SG6 — 7 F4
Howards Wood. SG6 — 7 E5
Hurst Clo. SG7 — 5 H2

Iceni Ct. SG6 — 4 C4
Icknield Grn. SG6 — 6 C2
Icknield Way,
  Baldock. SG7 — 5 F2
Icknield Way,
  Letchworth. SG6 — 4 A5
Icknield Way East,
  Baldock. SG7 — 5 G2

INDUSTRIAL & RETAIL:
Ascot Ind Est. SG6 — 4 C4
Business Centre East.
  SG6 — 4 D5
Business Centre West.
  SG6 — 4 D5
Cotton Brown Park.
  SG6 — 7 G1
Garden Square Shopping
  Centre. SG6 — 6 D2
Greenlane Ind Est. SG6 — 7 F1
Jubilee Trade Centre.
  SG6 — 7 G1
Letchworth Business &
  Retail Pk. SG6 — 4 D4
Marquis Business Centre.
  SG7 — 5 G2
Shaftesbury Ind Est.
  SG6 — 4 C4
Woodside Ind Park.
  SG6 — 7 F1

Iredale View. SG7 — 5 H2
Ivel Ct. SG6 — 7 F4
Ivel Way. SG7 — 5 H5

Jackmans Pl. SG6 — 7 F2
Jackson St. SG7 — 5 F2
Jarden. SG6 — 7 G4
Jay Clo. SG6 — 4 A3
Jeve Clo. SG7 — 5 H2
Jubilee Rd. SG6 — 7 G1

Kestrel Walk. SG6 — 7 F5
Kimberley. SG6 — 4 B1
Kite Way. SG6 — 6 C1
Knapp Clo. SG6 — 5 E3
Kristiansand Way. SG6 — 4 D3
Kyrkeby. SG6 — 7 G4

Lacerta Ct. SG6 — 5 E3
Lacre Way. SG6 — 7 G1
Lammas Way. SG6 — 4 B3
Lannock. SG6 — 7 G4
Lapwing Dell. SG6 — 7 F6
Larkins Clo. SG7 — 5 G2
Lavender Ct. SG7 — 5 F2
Lawrence Av. SG6 — 7 E4
Laxton Gdns. SG7 — 5 H4
Letchworth Gate. SG6 — 7 F3
Letchworth La. SG6 — 6 D5
Letchworth Rd. SG7 — 5 F3
Leys Av. SG6 — 6 D2
Limekiln Lane. SG7 — 5 H4
Linden Croft. SG6 — 4 B2
Linnet Clo. SG6 — 6 C1
London Rd. SG7 — 5 G5
Longmead. SG6 — 6 C1
Lordship La. SG6 — 7 E4
Lytton Av. SG6 — 6 D3

Maddles. SG6 — 7 H4
Maltings Clo. SG7 — 5 H3
Manor Clo. SG6 — 6 D5
Manor Way. SG6 — 6 D6
Mansfield Rd. SG7 — 5 F4
Marmet Av. SG6 — 6 C2
Martin Way. SG6 — 6 B3
Maycroft. SG6 — 4 B2
Meadow Way. SG6 — 6 D3
Meeting House La. SG7 — 5 F2
Mercia Rd. SG7 — 5 H3
Meredews. SG6 — 7 F1
Middlefields. SG6 — 4 B2
Midhurst. SG6 — 4 A3
Milne Clo. SG6 — 7 F5
Monklands. SG6 — 6 B2
Monks Clo. SG6 — 6 B2
Mons Av. SG7 — 5 G5
Muddy La. SG6 — 6 D5
Mullway. SG6 — 6 B2

Netley Dell. SG6 — 7 F5
Nevells Grn. SG6 — 4 B4
Nevells Rd. SG6 — 4 A5
Newells. SG6 — 7 E5
Newlands. SG6 — 7 E5
Nightingale Way. SG7 — 5 G5
Normans Clo. SG6 — 4 B2
North Av. SG6 — 4 C3
North Rd. SG7 — 5 F1
Northfields. SG6 — 4 A2
Norton Cres. SG7 — 5 F3
Norton Hall Farm. SG6 — 4 D2
Norton Rd. SG6 — 4 C3
Norton Rd. SG7 — 5 F3
Norton Way Nth. SG6 — 4 B4
Norton Way Sth. SG6 — 7 E4
Nortonbury Rd. SG6 — 4 D1

Oak Tree Clo. SG6 — 6 C4
Oakhill. SG6 — 7 H4
Olden Mead. SG6 — 7 F5
Openshaw Way. SG6 — 6 D2
Orchard Clo. SG6 — 4 A3